soup

simply sensational

matthew drennan's
soup
simply sensational

photographs by martin brigdale

aquamarine

For Ken Hassett with love, for courage under fire.

First published by Aquamarine in 2000
© 2000 Anness Publishing Limited

Aquamarine is an imprint of
Anness Publishing Inc.
27 West 20th Street
New York, NY 10011

Publisher	Joanna Lorenz
Executive Editor	Linda Fraser
Production Controller	Ann Childers
Editorial Reader	Diane Ashmore
Photographer	Martin Brigdale
Designer	Mark Latter
Stylist	Helen Trent
Home Economist	Maxine Clark
assisted by	Kate Harbeson, Kate Jay
	and Julie Beresford

contents

introduction

Soup has evolved in so many ways, and has continuously been reinvented over the centuries, from its early beginnings when mankind first began to cook, to its place of honor at today's fashionable soup bars.

It is likely that soup originated solely as a medium for cooking other ingredients. Meat and vegetables had to be boiled in plenty of water in order to soften them, and make them more palatable and safe to eat. Cooks soon discovered that the cooking liquid was a full-flavored byproduct and it was destined to become the food we now know as soup.

No other dish has transcended the class barriers in quite the same way as soup—it has always been eaten by everyone. The poor survived on a daily main meal of water thickened with oatmeal or bread, flavorer

with whatever meager vegetables or pulses the garden would provide. The rich ate a similar dish, but it was enriched with meat, cream, butter, herbs and even alcohol.

into a chilled soup of puréed melon? When flavors from Thai curries and noodle dishes are fused with soup-making methods, the results are hearty, spiced meals. The tagines and couscous dishes of Morocco also offer innovative ideas for fabulous new soups.

We live in an era where convenience and speed are paramount. Supermarkets and stores sell "homemade" soups, but most would agree that there is absolutely nothing to match the flavor of real homemade soup. It is much less expensive than bought soup, and the notion that making good soup takes experience or is time-consuming is a complete fallacy. The only key to success is starting with good ingredients.

Soup has come a long way since the days of such a culinary divide. We now have a global approach to cooking, and we sample the flavors of soups that exist all over the world. From the steaming broths of China and Japan, thick, creamy chowders of New England and refined purées of France and Britain—every cuisine has its classic soup.

Soup has crossed cultural boundaries and begged, borrowed or stolen characteristics from its gastronomic cousins. Until recently, who would have contemplated the idea of classic French moules marinière served as a robust soup, or an icy sorbet melting slowly

Stock plays a starring role in soup, yet we rely increasingly on convenient store-bought stock cubes. These are fine, particularly if the soup is strongly flavored, but a simple or delicately flavored soup benefits greatly from homemade stock. Stock may take some time to bubble gently and develop flavor, but it takes no time at all to prepare.

As you will discover in the following chapters, soups can be cooked to suit all occasions, all weathers and all appetites. This is one of the world's universal dishes that encompasses good eating and drinking—and that is what makes soup unique.

cool and chilled

Our passion for soup grows constantly, and its repertoire extends to suit even the warmest days. Juicy melons, cool cucumber and earthy beets are among summer's signature flavors that are ideal for cold soups.

iced melon soup
with melon and mint sorbet

you will need

5–5¼ pounds very ripe melon

3 tablespoons orange juice

2 tablespoons lemon juice

mint leaves, to garnish

FOR THE MELON AND MINT SORBET

2 tablespoons sugar

½ cup water

5–5¼ pounds very ripe melon

juice of 2 limes

2 tablespoons chopped fresh mint

Serves 6–8

Use different melons for the cool soup and sorbet to create a subtle contrast in flavor and color. Try a combination of Charentais and Ogen or cantaloupe and Galia.

1 To make the melon and mint sorbet, put the sugar and water into a saucepan and heat gently until the sugar dissolves. Bring to a boil and simmer for 4–5 minutes, then remove from heat and let cool.

2 Halve the melons. Scrape out the seeds, then cut into large wedges and cut the flesh out of the skin. Weigh 3–3½ pounds melon.

3 Purée the melon in a food processor or blender with the cooled syrup and lime juice.

4 Stir in the mint and pour the melon mixture into an ice-cream maker. Churn, following the manufacturer's instructions, until the sorbet is smooth and firm. Alternatively, pour the mixture into a suitable container and freeze until icy around the edges. Transfer to a food processor or blender and process until smooth. Repeat the freezing and processing two or three times or until smooth and holding its shape, then freeze until firm.

5 To make the chilled melon soup, prepare the melon as in step 2 and purée it in a food processor or blender. Pour the purée into a bowl and stir in the orange and lemon juice. Place the soup in the refrigerator for 30–40 minutes, but do not chill it for too long, as this will dull its flavor.

6 Ladle the soup into bowls and add a large scoop of the sorbet to each. Garnish with mint leaves and serve immediately.

classic gazpacho

A wonderful, traditional chilled soup from the kitchens of Spain that is as popular today as it was when first made centuries ago.

1 In a large bowl, mix the tomatoes, cucumber, peppers, garlic and onion. Stir in the vinegar, oil, bread crumbs and water until well mixed. Purée the mixture in a food processor or blender until almost smooth and pour into a large bowl. If the soup is too thick, add a little cold water. Stir in salt and pepper to taste and chill.

2 To make the garnish, heat the oil in a frying pan and add the bread cubes.

3 Cook over medium heat for 5–6 minutes, stirring occasionally to brown evenly. Drain on paper towels and put into a small bowl. Place the remaining garnish ingredients into separate bowls or onto a serving plate.

4 Ladle the gazpacho into bowls and add ice cubes to each, then serve immediately. Pass the bowls of garnish ingredients with the soup so that they can be added to taste.

you will need

2 pounds ripe tomatoes, peeled and seeded

1 cucumber, peeled and roughly chopped

2 red bell peppers, seeded and roughly chopped

2 garlic cloves, crushed

1 large onion, roughly chopped

2 tablespoons white wine vinegar

½ cup olive oil

4½ cups fresh white bread crumbs

scant 2 cups ice water

salt and ground black pepper

ice cubes, to serve

FOR THE GARNISH

2–3 tablespoons olive oil

4 thick slices bread, crusts removed and cut into small cubes

2 tomatoes, peeled, seeded and finely diced

1 small green bell pepper, seeded and finely diced

1 small onion, very finely sliced

small bunch of fresh flat-leaf parsley, chopped

Serves 6

roasted bell pepper soup
with hot parmesan toasts

The secret of this soup is to serve it just cold, not over-chilled, topped with hot Parmesan toasts.

1 Preheat the oven to 400°F. Put the onion, garlic and peppers in a roasting pan. Drizzle the oil over the vegetables and mix well, then turn the pieces of pepper skin-sides up. Roast for 25–30 minutes, until slightly charred, then allow to cool slightly.

2 Squeeze the garlic flesh into a food processor or blender. Add the roasted vegetables, orange zest and juice, tomatoes and water. Process until smooth, then press through a sieve into a bowl. Season well and chill for 30 minutes.

3 Make the Parmesan toasts when you are ready to serve the soup. Preheat the broiler to high. Tear the baguette in half lengthwise, then tear or cut it across into four large pieces. Spread the pieces of bread with butter.

4 Pare most of the Parmesan into thin slices or shavings using a swivel-bladed vegetable knife or a small paring knife, then finely grate the remainder. Arrange the sliced Parmesan on the toasts, then dredge with the grated cheese.

5 Transfer the cheese-topped baguette pieces to a large baking sheet or broiler pan and toast under the broiler for a few minutes, until the topping is well browned.

6 Ladle the chilled soup into large, shallow bowls and sprinkle with snipped fresh chives, if using, and plenty of freshly ground black pepper. Serve the hot Parmesan toasts with the chilled soup.

you will need

1 onion, quartered

4 garlic cloves, unpeeled

2 red bell peppers, seeded and quartered

2 yellow bell peppers, seeded and quartered

2–3 tablespoons olive oil

grated zest and juice of 1 orange

7-ounce can chopped tomatoes

2½ cups cold water

salt and ground black pepper

2 tablespoons snipped fresh chives,
to garnish (optional)

FOR THE HOT PARMESAN TOASTS

1 medium baguette

¼ cup butter

6 ounces Parmesan cheese

Serves 4

cook's tip

The easiest way to press the soup through a sieve is to use a mushroom-shaped wooden tool known as a champignon. However, if you don't have one, then use the bottom of a large ladle or the back of a wooden spoon instead.

spiced mango soup
with yogurt

you will need

2 ripe mangoes

1 tablespoon all-purpose flour

½ cup plain yogurt

3¾ cups cold water

½ teaspoon grated fresh ginger root

2 red chiles, seeded and finely chopped

2 tablespoons olive oil

½ teaspoon mustard seeds

½ teaspoon cumin seeds

8 curry leaves

salt and ground black pepper

fresh mint leaves, shredded, to garnish

plain yogurt, to serve

Serves 4

This delicious, light soup recipe comes from Chutney Mary's, an Anglo-Indian restaurant in London. It is best when served lightly chilled.

1 Peel the mangoes, remove the pits and cut the flesh into chunks. Purée in a food processor or blender until smooth. Pour into a saucepan and stir in the flour, yogurt, water, ginger and chiles. Bring slowly to a boil, stirring occasionally. Simmer for 4–5 minutes, until thickened slightly, then set aside off the heat.

2 Heat the oil in a frying pan. Add the mustard seeds and cook for a few seconds, until they begin to pop, then add the cumin seeds.

3 Add the curry leaves and then cook for 5 minutes. Stir the spice mixture into the soup, return it to the heat and cook for 10 minutes.

4 Press through a sieve, if desired, then season to taste. Let the soup cool completely, then chill for at least 1 hour.

5 Ladle the soup into bowls, and top each with a dollop of yogurt. Garnish with shredded mint leaves and serve.

cucumber and yogurt soup with chili salsa and salmon

The refreshing flavors of cucumber and yogurt in this soup fuse with the cool salsa and a hint of heat from the charred salmon to bring the taste of summer to the table.

1 Peel two of the cucumbers and halve them lengthwise. Scoop out and discard the seeds using a spoon, then roughly chop the flesh. Purée in a food processor or blender, then add the yogurt, stock, crème fraîche, chervil, chives and seasoning, and process until smooth. Chill.

2 Peel, halve and seed the remaining cucumber. Cut the flesh into small, neat dice. Mix with the chopped parsley and chilli. Chill until required.

3 Brush a griddle or frying pan with oil and heat until very hot. Sear the salmon slices for 1–2 minutes on each side, until tender and charred.

4 Ladle the chilled soup into soup bowls. Top with two slices of the salmon, then pile a portion of salsa into the center of each. Garnish with the chervil or chives and serve.

you will need

3 medium cucumbers

1¼ cups plain yogurt

1 cup vegetable stock, chilled

½ cup crème fraîche

1 tablespoon chopped
fresh chervil

1 tablespoon snipped fresh chives

1 tablespoon chopped fresh
flat-leaf parsley

1 small red chile, seeded and very
finely chopped

a little oil, for brushing

8 ounces salmon fillet, skinned
and cut into eight thin slices

salt and ground black pepper

fresh chervil or chives, to garnish

Serves 4

cherry tomato soup
with arugula pesto

you will need

8 ounces cherry tomatoes, halved

8 ounces plum tomatoes, halved

8 ounces vine-ripened tomatoes, halved

2 shallots, roughly chopped

1½ tablespoons sun-dried tomato paste

2½ cups vegetable stock

salt and ground black pepper

ice cubes, to serve

FOR THE ARUGULA PESTO

½ ounce arugula leaves

5 tablespoons olive oil

2 tablespoons pine nuts

1 garlic clove

⅓ cup freshly grated
Parmesan cheese

Serves 4

For their size, cherry tomatoes are a powerhouse of sweetness and flavor. Here they are complemented beautifully by a rich paste of peppery arugula.

1 Purée all the tomatoes and shallots in a food processor or blender. Add the sun-dried tomato paste and process until smooth. Press the purée through a sieve into a saucepan.

2 Add the vegetable stock and heat gently for 4–5 minutes. Season well. Let cool, then chill for at least 4 hours.

3 For the arugula pesto, put the arugula, oil, pine nuts and garlic in a food processor or blender and process to form a paste. Transfer to a bowl and stir in the Parmesan cheese. (This can also be prepared using a mortar and pestle.)

4 Ladle the soup into bowls and add a few ice cubes to each. Spoon some of the arugula pesto into the center of each portion and serve.

variation

The pesto can be made with other soft-leaved herbs instead of arugula. Try fresh basil, cilantro or mint, or use a mixture of herbs, if desired. Parsley and mint are a good flavor combination and make delicious pesto.

vichyssoise
with watercress cream

Soups may have entered a brave new world, but there are classic old-timers, such as this cold French version of leek and potato soup, that will remain favorites.

1 Melt the butter in a large saucepan. Add the onion and leeks, cover and cook gently for 10 minutes, stirring occasionally, until softened. Stir in the potatoes and stock, and bring to a boil. Reduce the heat and simmer for 20 minutes or until the potatoes are tender. Cool slightly.

2 Process the soup in a food processor or blender until smooth, then press through a sieve into a clean bowl.

3 Stir in the milk and light cream. Season the soup well and chill for at least 2 hours.

4 To make the watercress cream, process the watercress in a food processor or blender until finely chopped, then stir in the chervil and cream. Pour into a bowl and stir in the nutmeg with seasoning to taste. Ladle the vichyssoise into bowls and spoon the watercress cream on top. Garnish with chervil and serve.

you will need

¼ cup butter

1 onion, sliced

1 pound leeks, sliced

8 ounces potatoes, sliced

3 cups chicken stock

1¼ cups milk

3 tablespoons light cream

salt and ground black pepper

fresh chervil, to garnish

FOR THE WATERCRESS CREAM

1 bunch watercress, about 3 ounces, stems removed

small bunch of fresh chervil, finely chopped

⅔ cup heavy cream

pinch of freshly grated nutmeg

Serves 6

you will need

2 tablespoons butter

1 leek, sliced

1 garlic clove, crushed

4 cups frozen petits pois

5 cups vegetable stock

small bunch of fresh chives,
coarsely snipped

1¼ cups heavy cream

6 tablespoons plain yogurt

4 slices prosciutto, roughly chopped

salt and ground black pepper

fresh chives, to garnish

Serves 6

summer pea and chive soup with prosciutto

This quick and simple soup is light and refreshing. Using frozen petits pois eliminates the labor involved in shelling fresh peas without compromising the flavor.

1 Melt the butter in a saucepan. Add the leek and garlic, cover and cook gently for 4–5 minutes, until softened. Stir in the petits pois, stock and chives. Bring slowly to a boil, then simmer for 5 minutes. Cool slightly.

2 Process the soup in a food processor or blender until smooth. Pour into a bowl, stir in the cream and season. Chill for at least 2 hours.

3 Ladle the soup into bowls and add a spoon-ful of yogurt to the center of each. Sprinkle the chopped prosciutto on top and garnish with chives before serving.

cook's tip

For a clever garnish, cut five lengths of chive to about 2½ inches, then use another chive to tie them together. Lay this on top of the soup.

avocado and lime soup
with a green chili salsa

Inspired by guacamole, the popular avocado dip, this creamy soup relies on good-quality ripe avocados for its flavor and color.

1 Prepare the salsa first. Mix all the ingredients and season well. Chill until needed.

2 Halve and pit the avocados. Scoop the flesh out of the avocado skins and place in a food processor or blender. Add the lime juice, garlic, ice cubes and ⅔ cup of the vegetable stock.

3 Process the soup until smooth. Pour into a large bowl and stir in the remaining stock, milk, sour cream, Tabasco and seasoning.

4 Ladle the soup into bowls or glasses and spoon a little salsa on top. Add a splash of olive oil to each portion and garnish with cilantro leaves. Serve immediately.

you will need

3 ripe avocados
juice of 1½ limes
1 garlic clove, crushed
handful of ice cubes
1⅔ cups vegetable stock, chilled
1⅔ cups milk, chilled
⅔ cup sour cream, chilled
few drops of Tabasco
salt and ground black pepper
cilantro leaves, to garnish
extra virgin olive oil, to serve

FOR THE SALSA

4 tomatoes, peeled, seeded and
finely diced
2 scallions, finely chopped
1 green chile, seeded and
finely chopped
1 tablespoon chopped cilantro
juice of ½ lime

Serves 4

cook's tips

It is easy to remove the pit from an avocado. Halve the avocado and simply tap the pit firmly with the edge of a large knife. Twist the knife gently and the pit will pop out.

This soup may discolor if left standing for too long, but the flavor will not be spoiled. Give it a quick whisk just before serving.

beet and cranberry soup with mascarpone brioche

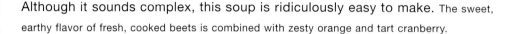

you will need

12 ounces cooked beets, roughly chopped

grated zest and juice of 1 orange

2½ cups unsweetened cranberry juice

scant 2 cups plain yogurt

a little Tabasco

4 slices brioche

4 tablespoons mascarpone

salt and ground black pepper

fresh mint sprigs and cooked cranberries, to garnish

Serves 4

Although it sounds complex, this soup is ridiculously easy to make. The sweet, earthy flavor of fresh, cooked beets is combined with zesty orange and tart cranberry.

1 Purée the beets with the orange zest and juice, half the cranberry juice and the yogurt in a food processor or blender until smooth.

2 Press the purée through a sieve into a clean bowl. Stir in the remaining cranberry juice, Tabasco and salt and pepper to taste. Chill for at least 2 hours.

3 Preheat the broiler. Using a large cookie cutter, stamp a round out of each slice of brioche and toast until golden. Ladle the soup into bowls and top each with a brioche slice and a dollop of mascarpone. Garnish with mint and fresh cranberries.

cook's tip

If the oranges you use are a little tart, add a pinch or two of sugar to the soup.

tomato and peach jus
with butterflied shrimp

Soups, made from the clear juices extracted from vegetables or fruits and referred to as "water" soups by chefs, provide the inspiration for this recipe.

1 Purée the peaches and tomatoes in a food processor or blender. Stir in the vinegar and seasoning to taste. Line a large sieve with muslin. Pour the purée into the bowl, gather up the ends of the muslin and tie tightly. Suspend over the bowl and let stand at room temperature for 3 hours or until about 5 cups of juice have drained through.

2 Meanwhile, put the lemongrass, ginger and bay leaf into a saucepan with the water, and simmer for 5–6 minutes. Set aside to cool. Strain the mixture into the tomato and peach juice and chill for at least 4 hours.

3 Using a sharp knife, slit the shrimp down their curved sides, cutting about three-quarters of the way through and keeping their tails intact. Open them out flat.

4 Heat a griddle or frying pan and brush with a little oil. Sear the shrimp for 1–2 minutes on each side, until tender and slightly charred. Pat dry on paper towels to remove any remaining oil. Cool, but do not chill.

5 Ladle the soup into bowls and place three shrimp in each portion.

you will need

3–3½ pounds ripe peaches, peeled, pitted and cut into chunks

2½ pounds beef tomatoes, peeled and cut into chunks

2 tablespoons white wine vinegar

1 lemongrass stalk, crushed and chopped

1-inch piece fresh ginger root, grated

1 bay leaf

⅔ cup water

18 tiger shrimp, shelled with tails on and deveined

olive oil, for brushing

salt and ground black pepper

handful of cilantro leaves and 2 vine-ripened tomatoes, peeled, seeded and diced, to garnish

Serves 6

east meets west

Fusion is the buzz word in cooking today, and soup is no exception. The subtle and hot flavors from the countries in Southeast Asia are blended with the tastes, techniques and ingredients of the Americas and Europe.

sweet-and-sour pork soup

This very quick, sharp and tangy soup is perfect for an impromptu supper. It can also be made with shredded chicken breast instead of pork.

1 Cut the pork into very fine strips, 2 inches in length. Mix with the papaya and set aside. Process the shallots, crushed peppercorns, garlic and shrimp paste together in a food processor or blender to form a paste.

2 Heat the oil in a heavy saucepan and fry the paste for 1–2 minutes. Add the stock and bring to a boil. Reduce the heat. Add the pork and papaya, ginger and tamarind water. Simmer for 7–8 minutes, until the pork is tender.

3 Stir in the honey, lime juice, most of the chiles and scallions. Season to taste. Ladle the soup into bowls and serve immediately, garnished with the remaining chiles and onions.

you will need

2 pounds pork fillet, trimmed

1 unripe papaya, halved, seeded, peeled and shredded

3 shallots, chopped

1 teaspoon crushed black peppercorns

5 garlic cloves, chopped

1 tablespoon shrimp paste

2 tablespoons vegetable oil

6¼ cups chicken stock

1-inch piece fresh ginger root, grated

½ cup tamarind water

1 tablespoon honey

juice of 1 lime

2 small red chiles, seeded and sliced

4 scallions, sliced

salt and ground black pepper

Serves 6–8

smoked haddock chowder with sweet thai basil

Based on a traditional Scottish recipe, this soup has sweetness from the sweet potatoes and butternut squash, and is flavored with a hint of Thai basil.

1 Cook the sweet potatoes and butternut squash separately in boiling salted water for 15 minutes or until just tender. Drain both well.

2 Meanwhile, melt half the butter in a large, heavy saucepan. Add the onion and cook for 4–5 minutes, until softened but not browned. Add the haddock fillets and water.

3 Bring to a boil, reduce the heat and simmer for 10 minutes, until the fish is cooked. Use a draining spoon to lift the fish out of the pan and let cool. Set the cooking liquid aside.

4 When cool enough to handle, carefully break the flesh into large flakes, discarding the skin and bones. Set the fish aside.

5 Press the sweet potatoes through a sieve and beat in the remaining butter with seasoning to taste. Strain the reserved fish cooking liquid and return it to the rinsed-out pan, then whisk in the sweet potato. Stir in the milk and bring to a boil. Simmer for 2–3 minutes.

6 Stir in the butternut squash, fish, Thai basil leaves and cream. Season the soup to taste and heat through without boiling. Ladle the soup into six warmed soup bowls and serve immediately.

you will need

14 ounces sweet potatoes (pink-fleshed variety), cut into small bite-size pieces
8 ounces peeled butternut squash, cut into ½-inch slices
¼ cup butter
1 onion, chopped
1 pound Finnan haddock fillets, skinned
1¼ cups water
2½ cups milk
small handful of Thai basil leaves
¼ cup heavy cream
salt and ground black pepper

Serves 6

thai chicken noodle soup
with little crab cakes

This soup is a meal in itself. Look for stores that sell bunches of cilantro with the roots still attached, as the roots add excellent flavor to the stock.

you will need

8 garlic cloves

small bunch of cilantro, with roots on

2½–3 pounds chicken

2 star anise

2 carrots, chopped

2 celery stalks, chopped

1 onion, chopped

2 tablespoons soy sauce

5 ounces egg noodles

2 tablespoons vegetable oil

¼ cup Thai fish sauce (*nam pla*)

¼ teaspoon chili powder

1½ cups bean sprouts

2 scallions, sliced

herb sprigs, to garnish

salt and ground black pepper

FOR THE CRAB CAKES

1 teaspoon Thai red curry paste

1 teaspoon cornstarch

1 teaspoon Thai fish sauce (*nam pla*)

1 small egg yolk

1 tablespoon chopped cilantro

6 ounces white crabmeat

1 cup fresh white bread crumbs

2 tablespoons vegetable oil

Serves 6

1 Chop four of the garlic cloves, then thinly slice the remainder and set them aside. Cut the roots off the cilantro stems and place in a large, heavy saucepan with the chopped garlic. Pick the cilantro leaves off their stems and set them aside; discard the stems. Place the chicken in the pan and add the star anise, carrots, celery and onion and soy sauce. Pour in enough water to just cover the chicken. Bring to a boil, reduce the heat, then cover and simmer for 1 hour.

2 To prepare the crab cakes, mix the curry paste, cornstarch, fish sauce and egg yolk in a bowl. Add the cilantro, crabmeat, bread crumbs and seasoning, then mix well. Divide the mixture into 12 portions and form each into a small cake.

3 Cook the egg noodles according to the package instructions. Drain and set aside. Heat the oil in a small pan and fry the sliced garlic until golden brown. Drain and set aside.

4 Remove the chicken from its stock and set aside until cool enough to handle. (Reserve the stock.) Discard the skin, take the meat off the bones and tear it into large strips. Set aside. Strain the stock and pour 5 cups into a large saucepan. Stir in the fish sauce, chili powder and seasoning, then bring to a boil. Reduce the heat and keep hot.

5 To cook the crab cakes, heat the vegetable oil in a large frying pan and fry the crab cakes for 2–3 minutes on each side until golden.

6 Divide the cooked noodles, fried garlic slices, bean sprouts, sliced scallions and chicken strips among six shallow soup bowls.

7 Arrange two of the crab cakes on top of the noodles, then ladle the hot chicken broth into the bowls. Sprinkle a few cilantro leaves on the soups, then garnish with the herb sprigs and serve immediately.

soup niçoise
with seared tuna

you will need

12 drained bottled anchovy fillets

2 tablespoons milk

4 ounces green beans, halved

4 plum tomatoes, peeled, halved and seeded

16 black olives, pitted

4 cups good vegetable stock

3 garlic cloves, crushed

2 tablespoons lemon juice

1 tablespoon olive oil

4 tuna steaks, about 3 ounces each

small bunch of scallions, shredded lengthwise

handful of fresh basil leaves, shredded

salt and ground black pepper

fresh crusty bread, to serve

Serves 4

Ingredients for the famous salad from Nice in the south of France are transformed into a simple yet elegant soup by adding a hot garlic-infused stock.

1 Soak the anchovies in the milk for 10 minutes. Drain well and dry on paper towels. Cook the green beans in boiling salted water for 2–3 minutes. Drain, refresh under cold running water and drain. Split any thick beans diagonally lengthwise. Cut the tomatoes into thin wedges. Wash the olives to remove any oil, then cut into quarters. Set all the prepared ingredients aside.

2 Bring the stock to a boil in a large, heavy saucepan. Add the garlic, reduce the heat and simmer for 10 minutes. Season the stock well and add the lemon juice.

3 Meanwhile, brush a griddle pan or frying pan with the oil and heat until very hot. Season the tuna and cook for about 2 minutes on each side. Do not overcook the tuna, or it will become dry.

4 Gently toss together the green beans, tomatoes, scallions, anchovies, black olives and shredded basil leaves.

5 Put the seared tuna steaks into four shallow bowls and pile the vegetable mixture on top. Carefully ladle the hot garlic stock around the ingredients. Serve immediately, with crusty bread.

cook's tip

Buy anchovy fillets that have been bottled in extra virgin olive oil if you can, as they have a superior flavor to the smaller anchovy fillets.

wonton, bok choy and shrimp tail soup

A well-flavored chicken stock or broth is a must for this classic Chinese snack, which is popular on fast-food stalls in towns and cities throughout Southern China.

1 Put the pork, shrimp, rice wine or sherry, soy sauce and sesame oil in a large bowl. Add plenty of seasoning and mix the ingredients.

2 Put about 2 teaspoons of pork mixture in the center of each wonton wrapper. Bring up the sides of the wrapper and pinch them together to seal the filling in a small bundle.

3 Bring a large saucepan of water to a boil. Add the wontons and cook for 3 minutes, then drain well and set aside.

4 Pour the stock into a large saucepan and bring to a boil. Season to taste. Add the tiger shrimp and cook for 2–3 minutes, until just tender. Add the wontons and bok choy, then cook for another 1–2 minutes. Ladle the soup into bowls and garnish with scallions and ginger.

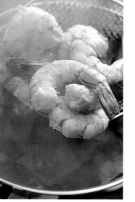

you will need

7 ounces ground pork

7 ounces cooked, peeled shrimp, thawed if frozen

2 teaspoons rice wine or dry sherry

2 teaspoons light soy sauce

1 teaspoon sesame oil

24 thin wonton wrappers

5 cups chicken stock

12 tiger shrimp, shelled, with tails still on

12 ounces bok choy, coarsely shredded

salt and ground black pepper

4 scallions, sliced and ½-inch piece fresh ginger root, finely shredded, to garnish

Serves 4

chicken and coconut soup
with crispy shallots

This recipe combines the flavors of Thailand in a smooth European-style soup, and the finished dish is complemented by a topping of crisp shallots.

1 Melt the butter in a large, heavy saucepan. Add the onion, garlic and ginger, then cook for 4–5 minutes, until softened. Stir in the curry paste and turmeric, and cook for another 2–3 minutes, stirring continuously.

2 Pour in two-thirds of the coconut milk; cook for 5 minutes. Add the stock, lime leaves, lemongrass and chicken. Heat until simmering; cook for 15 minutes or until the chicken is tender.

3 Use a draining spoon to remove the chicken thighs and set them aside to cool.

4 Add the spinach to the pan and cook for 3–4 minutes. Stir in the remaining coconut milk and seasoning, then process the soup in a food processor or blender until almost smooth. Return the soup to the rinsed-out pan. Cut the chicken thighs into bite-size pieces and stir these into the soup with the fish sauce and lime juice.

5 Reheat the soup gently until hot, but do not let it boil. Meanwhile, heat the oil in a frying pan and cook the shallots for 6–8 minutes, until crisp and golden, stirring occasionally. Drain on paper towels. Ladle the soup into bowls, then top with the basil leaves and fried shallots, and serve.

you will need

3 tablespoons butter

1 onion, finely chopped

2 garlic cloves, chopped

1-inch piece fresh ginger root, finely chopped

2 teaspoons Thai green curry paste

½ teaspoon turmeric

14-fluid ounce can coconut milk

2 cups chicken stock

2 lime leaves, shredded

1 lemongrass stalk, finely chopped

8 skinless, boneless chicken thighs

12 ounces spinach, roughly chopped

2 teaspoons Thai fish sauce (*nam pla*)

2 tablespoons lime juice

2 tablespoons vegetable oil

2 shallots, thinly sliced

small handful of Thai purple basil leaves

salt and ground black pepper

Serves 6

tomato soup
with chili squid and tarragon

Asian-style seared squid mingles with the pungent tomato and garlic flavors of the Mediterranean in this superlative soup.

you will need

4 small squid (or 1–2 large squid)

4 tablespoons olive oil

2 shallots, chopped

1 garlic clove, crushed

2½ pounds ripe tomatoes, roughly chopped

1 tablespoon sun-dried tomato paste

scant 2 cups vegetable stock

about ½ teaspoon sugar

2 red chiles, seeded and chopped

2 tablespoons chopped fresh tarragon

salt and ground black pepper

crusty bread, to serve

Serves 4

2 Cut the squid into rings and set these aside with the tentacles.

3 Heat 2 tablespoons of the oil in a saucepan. Add the shallots and garlic, and cook for 4–5 minutes, until just softened. Stir in the tomatoes and tomato paste, and season. Cover and cook for 3 minutes. Add half the stock and simmer for 5 minutes, until the tomatoes are very soft.

4 Cool the soup, then rub it through a sieve and return it to the rinsed-out saucepan. Stir in the remaining stock and sugar, and reheat gently.

1 Wash the squid under cold running water. To clean it, grasp the head and tentacles in one hand and pull the body away with the other. Discard the intestines that come away with the head. Cut the tentacles away from the head in one piece and reserve them; discard the head. Pull the plastic-like quill out of the main body and remove any roe that may be present. Pull off the fins from either side of the body pouch and rub off the semi-transparent, mottled skin. Wash the prepared squid under cold running water.

5 Meanwhile, heat the remaining oil in a large frying pan. Add the squid rings and tentacles, and the chiles. Cook for 4–5 minutes, stirring continuously, then remove from heat and stir in the chopped tarragon.

6 Taste the soup and adjust the seasoning if necessary. If the soup tastes slightly sharp, add a little extra sugar. Ladle the soup into four bowls and spoon the chili squid in the center. Serve immediately with crusty bread.

duck broth with orange spiced dumplings

Using a delicate touch when stirring the mixture for the dumplings will lead to a light texture to match their delicious flavor.

you will need

1 duckling, 4–4½ pounds, with liver

1 large onion, halved

2 carrots, thickly sliced

½ garlic bulb

1 bouquet garni

3 cloves

2 tablespoons snipped chives, to garnish

FOR THE SPICED DUMPLINGS

2 thick slices white bread

¼ cup milk

2 strips bacon

1 shallot, finely chopped

1 garlic clove, crushed

1 egg yolk, beaten

grated zest of 1 orange

½ teaspoon paprika

½ cup all-purpose flour

salt and ground black pepper

Serves 4

1 Set the duck liver aside. Using a sharp knife, cut off the breasts from the duckling and set them aside. Put the duck carcass into a large, heavy saucepan and pour in enough water to cover the carcass completely. Bring to a boil and skim the scum off the surface.

2 Add the onion, carrots, garlic, bouquet garni and cloves. Reduce the heat and cover the pan, then simmer for 2 hours, skimming occasionally to remove any scum.

3 Lift the carcass from the broth and let cool. Strain the broth, and skim it to remove any fat. Return the broth to the pan and simmer gently, uncovered, until reduced to 5 cups.

4 Remove all meat from the duck carcass and shred it finely, then set it aside.

5 To make the dumplings, soak the bread in the milk for 5 minutes. Remove the skin and fat from the duck breasts. Grind the meat with the duck liver and bacon. Squeeze the milk from the bread, then add the bread to the ground meat with the shallot, garlic, egg yolk, orange zest, paprika, flour and seasoning, and mix.

6 Form a spoonful of the mixture into a ball, a little smaller than a walnut. Repeat with the remaining mixture to make 20 small dumplings. Bring a large saucepan of lightly salted water to a boil and poach the dumplings for 4–5 minutes, until just tender.

7 Bring the duck broth back to a boil and add the dumplings. Divide the shredded duck meat among four bowls and ladle in the broth and dumplings. Garnish with chives.

shiitake mushroom and red onion laksa

"Noodles" of finely sliced red onions enhance the traditional flour noodles in this soup, which is based on the classic soup, Penang laksa.

1 Place the mushrooms in a bowl and pour in enough boiling stock to cover them, then let soak for 30 minutes. Put the tamarind paste into a bowl and pour in the hot water. Mash the paste against the side of the bowl with a fork to extract as much flavor as possible, then strain and reserve the liquid, discarding the pulp.

2 Soak the chiles in hot water to cover for 5 minutes, then drain, reserving the liquid.

3 Process the lemongrass, turmeric, galangal, onion, soaked chiles and shrimp paste in a food processor or blender, adding a little soaking water from the chiles to form a paste.

4 Heat the oil in a large, heavy saucepan and cook the paste over low heat for 4–5 minutes, until fragrant. Add the tamarind liquid and bring to a boil, then simmer for 5 minutes. Remove from heat.

you will need

2½ cups dried shiitake mushrooms
5 cups boiling vegetable stock
2 tablespoons tamarind paste
1 cup hot water
6 large dried red chiles, stems removed and seeded
2 lemongrass stalks, finely sliced
1 teaspoon ground turmeric
1 tablespoon grated fresh galangal
1 onion, chopped
1 teaspoon dried shrimp paste
2 tablespoons oil
2 teaspoons sugar
6 ounces rice vermicelli
1 red onion, very finely sliced
1 small cucumber, seeded and cut into strips
handful of fresh mint leaves, to garnish

Serves 6

5 Drain the mushrooms and reserve the stock. Discard the stems, then halve or quarter the mushrooms, if large. Add the mushrooms to the pan with their soaking liquid, the remaining stock and the sugar. Simmer for 25–30 minutes or until the mushrooms are tender.

6 Put the rice vermicelli into a large bowl and cover with boiling water, then let soak for 4 minutes or according to the package instructions. Drain well, then divide among six bowls. Top with onion and cucumber, then ladle in the boiling shiitake soup. Add a small bunch of mint leaves to each bowl and serve immediately.

jamaican rice and pea soup
with salt cod

Based on the classic Caribbean dish of rice and peas, this recipe is made with black-eyed peas, but kidney beans or, more traditionally, pigeon peas can be used instead.

1 Heat the oil and 2 tablespoons of the butter in a large, heavy saucepan. Add the bacon and cook for 3–4 minutes, until golden. Stir in the onion, garlic and chile and cook for another 4–5 minutes.

2 Stir in the rice and cook for 1–2 minutes, until the grains are translucent. Stir in the thyme, cinnamon stick and black-eyed peas and cook for 1–2 minutes. Pour in the water and bring to a boil. Reduce the heat to low and cook for 25–30 minutes.

3 Meanwhile, wash the soaked salt cod under cold running water. Pat dry with paper towels and remove the skin. Cut into bite-size pieces and toss in the flour until evenly coated. Shake off the excess flour.

4 Melt the remaining butter in a large, heavy frying pan. Add the cod, in batches if necessary, and cook for 4–5 minutes, until tender and golden. Remove the cod and set aside.

5 Stir the coconut milk into the cooked rice and beans. Remove the cinnamon stick and cook the soup for 2–3 minutes. Stir in the spinach and cook for another 2–3 minutes. Add the cod and chopped parsley, season and heat through. Ladle the soup into bowls and serve.

cook's tip

Lardons are neat strips of fatty meat, such as pork belly or bacon. They are thicker and slightly longer than matchsticks. Cut them from very thick strips of bacon.

you will need

1 tablespoon sunflower oil

6 tablespoons butter

4 ounces thick bacon, cut into lardons

1 onion, chopped

2 garlic cloves, chopped

1 red chile, seeded and chopped

generous 1 cup long-grain rice

2 sprigs fresh thyme

1 cinnamon stick

14-ounce can black-eyed peas, drained and rinsed

3¾ cups water

12 ounces salt cod, soaked for 24 hours, changing the water several times

all-purpose flour, for dusting

14-fluid ounce can coconut milk

6 ounces baby spinach leaves

2 tablespoons chopped fresh parsley, to garnish

salt and ground black pepper

Serves 6

hot and spicy

Searing hot Mexican chiles, North African spices and pungent, aromatic flavors from Malaysia are just part of the powerhouse team behind these fiery soups. Increase the chiles and turn up the heat, if you dare.

curried parsnip soup
with sesame naan croutons

The mild sweetness of parsnips and mango chutney are given an exciting lift with a blend of spices in this simple soup.

1 Heat the oil in a large saucepan and add the onion, garlic, chile and ginger. Cook for 4–5 minutes, until the onion has softened. Add the parsnips and cook for 2–3 minutes. Sprinkle in the cumin seeds, coriander and turmeric, and cook for 1 minute, stirring constantly.

2 Add the chutney and the water. Season well and bring to a boil. Reduce the heat and simmer for 15 minutes, until the parsnips are soft.

3 Cool the soup slightly, then process it in a food processor or blender until smooth, and return it to the saucepan. Stir in the lime juice.

4 To make the naan croutons, heat the oil in a large frying pan and cook the diced naan for 3–4 minutes, stirring, until golden all over. Remove from heat and drain off any excess oil. Add the sesame seeds and return to the heat for 30 seconds, until the seeds are pale golden.

5 Ladle the soup into bowls. Spoon a little yogurt into each portion, then top with a little mango chutney and some of the sesame naan crouton mixture. Garnish with chopped cilantro, if desired.

you will need

2 tablespoons olive oil

1 onion, chopped

1 garlic clove, crushed

1 small green chile, seeded and finely chopped

1 tablespoon grated fresh ginger root

5 large parsnips, diced

1 teaspoon cumin seeds

1 teaspoon ground coriander

½ teaspoon ground turmeric

2 tablespoons mango chutney

5 cups water

juice of 1 lime

salt and ground black pepper

4 tablespoons plain yogurt and mango chutney, to serve

chopped cilantro, to garnish (optional)

FOR THE SESAME NAAN CROUTONS

3 tablespoons olive oil

1 large naan, cut into small dice

1 tablespoon sesame seeds

Serves 4

golden chorizo and chickpea soup

Small uncooked chorizo sausages are available at Spanish food stores, but ready-to-eat chorizo can be cut into chunks and used instead.

1 Place the chickpeas in a large saucepan. Cover with plenty of fresh water and bring to a boil, skimming off any scum as it forms. Cover and simmer for 2–3 hours, until tender. Add more boiling water, if necessary, to keep the chickpeas well covered during cooking. Drain, reserving the cooking liquid. Soak the saffron threads in a little warm water.

2 Heat the oil in a large, deep frying pan. Add the chorizo sausages and fry over medium heat for 5 minutes, until a lot of oil has seeped out of the sausages and they are pale golden brown. Drain and set aside.

3 Add the chile flakes and garlic to the fat in the pan and cook for a few seconds. Stir in the saffron with its soaking water, tomatoes, chickpeas, potatoes, chorizo sausages and bay leaves. Pour in a scant 2 cups of the chickpea cooking liquid and the water, and stir in salt and pepper to taste.

4 Bring to a boil, then reduce the heat and simmer for 45–50 minutes, stirring occasionally, until the potatoes are tender and the soup has thickened slightly.

5 Add the chopped parsley to the soup and adjust the seasoning. Ladle the soup into four large, warmed soup plates and drizzle a little extra virgin olive oil on each portion. Serve with crusty bread.

you will need

⅔ cup dried chickpeas, soaked overnight and drained

pinch of saffron threads

3 tablespoons olive oil

1 pound uncooked mini chorizo sausages

1 teaspoon dried chile flakes

6 garlic cloves, finely chopped

1 pound tomatoes, roughly chopped

12 ounces new potatoes, quartered

2 bay leaves

scant 2 cups water

¼ cup chopped fresh parsley

salt and ground black pepper

2 tablespoons extra virgin olive oil, to garnish

crusty bread, to serve

Serves 4

crab and chili soup
with cilantro relish

Prepared fresh crab is readily available, high quality and convenient—perfect for creating an exotic soup in minutes. Here it is accompanied by a hot cilantro and chili relish.

1 Heat the oil in a saucepan and add the onion, chiles and garlic. Cook over low heat for 10 minutes, until the onion is very soft. Transfer this mixture to a bowl and stir in the crabmeat, parsley, cilantro and lemon juice, then set aside.

2 Lay the lemongrass on a cutting board and bruise it with a rolling pin or pestle. Pour the stock and fish sauce into a saucepan. Add the lemongrass and bring to a boil, then add the pasta. Simmer, uncovered, for 3–4 minutes or according to the package instructions, until the pasta is just tender.

you will need

3 tablespoons olive oil

1 red onion, finely chopped

2 red chiles, seeded and finely chopped

1 garlic clove, finely chopped

1 pound fresh white crabmeat

2 tablespoons chopped fresh parsley

2 tablespoons chopped cilantro

juice of 2 lemons

1 lemongrass stalk

4 cups good fish or chicken stock

1 tablespoon Thai fish sauce *(nam pla)*

5 ounces vermicelli or angel hair pasta, broken into 2–3 inch lengths

salt and ground black pepper

FOR THE CILANTRO RELISH

1 cup cilantro leaves

1 green chile, seeded and chopped

1 tablespoon sunflower oil

1½ tablespoons lemon juice

½ teaspoon ground roasted cumin seeds

Serves 4

3 Meanwhile, make the cilantro relish. Place the cilantro, chile, oil, lemon juice and cumin in a food processor or blender and process to form a coarse paste (or use a mortar and pestle). Add seasoning to taste.

4 Remove and discard the lemongrass from the soup. Stir the chili and crab mixture into the soup and season it well. Bring to a boil, then reduce the heat and simmer for 2 minutes.

5 Ladle the soup into four deep, warmed bowls and put a spoonful of the relish in the center of each. Serve immediately.

chicken
and tiger shrimp laksa

Laksa is a spicy Malaysian noodle soup enriched with coconut milk. The ingredients can be as varied as you want, and the result is a substantial meal in itself.

1 Soak the chiles in hot water for 45 minutes. Cook the vermicelli in boiling water according to the package instructions. Drain and set aside.

2 Drain the chiles and put them in a food processor or blender with the shrimp paste, shallots, garlic, lemongrass, nuts, lime zest and juice. Process to form a thick paste.

3 Heat 3 tablespoons of the oil in a large, heavy saucepan. Add the spice paste and cook for 1–2 minutes, stirring continuously. Add the turmeric and coriander and cook for another 2 minutes. Stir in the stock and simmer gently, uncovered, for about 25 minutes, until slightly reduced. Strain the stock and set it aside. Heat the remaining oil in the rinsed-out saucepan.

4 Add the shrimp and cook for 2–3 minutes, until just tender. Use a draining spoon to remove the shrimp from the pan and set them aside. Add the chicken to the hot oil and cook for 4–5 minutes, until just cooked.

5 Pour in the flavored stock and the coconut milk, then taste for seasoning and reheat gently, but do not boil. Add the vermicelli and shrimp, and heat gently for 2 minutes. Stir in the bean sprouts, cucumber and scallions. Remove from heat, garnish with scallions and serve immediately with lime wedges.

cook's tip

Lemongrass, as the name implies, has a fragrant, lemon flavor and is popular in Thai and Malaysian cooking. To prepare, remove the outer layer and chop the lower 2 inches. The top end can be used to infuse flavor; simply bruise the stem and add to stock or soup.

you will need

6 dried red chiles, seeded

8 ounces vermicelli, broken into short lengths

1 tablespoon shrimp paste

10 shallots, chopped

3 garlic cloves

1 lemongrass stalk, roughly chopped (see cook's tip)

¼ cup macadamia nuts

grated zest and juice of 1 lime

4 tablespoons peanut oil

½ teaspoon ground turmeric

1 teaspoon ground coriander

6¼ cups fish or chicken stock

1 pound uncooked tiger shrimp,
shelled and deveined

1 pound skinless, boneless chicken breast, cut into long
thin strips

2 14-fluid ounce cans coconut milk

1 cup bean sprouts

½ cucumber, cut into matchstick strips

small bunch of scallions, shredded, plus extra
to garnish

salt and ground black pepper

1 lime, cut into wedges, to serve

Serves 6

indian-style lamb soup with rice and coconut

you will need

2 onions, chopped

6 garlic cloves, crushed

2-inch piece fresh ginger root, grated

6 tablespoons olive oil

2 tablespoons black poppy seeds

1 teaspoon cumin seeds

1 teaspoon coriander seeds

½ teaspoon ground turmeric

1 pound boneless lamb chops, trimmed and cut into bite-size pieces

¼ teaspoon cayenne pepper

5 cups lamb stock

generous ⅓ cup long-grain rice

2 tablespoons lemon juice

¼ cup coconut milk

salt and ground black pepper

cilantro sprigs and toasted shredded coconut, to garnish

Serves 6

This meaty soup thickened with long-grain rice is based on the classic Indian mulligatawny soup.

1 Process the onions, garlic, ginger and 1 tablespoon of the oil in a food processor or blender to form a paste. Set aside.

2 Heat a small, heavy frying pan. Add the poppy, cumin and coriander seeds and toast for a few seconds, until aromatic. Transfer the seeds to a mortar and grind them to a powder with a pestle. Stir in the turmeric. Set aside.

3 Heat the rest of the oil in a heavy saucepan. Fry the lamb in batches over high heat for 4–5 minutes, until browned all over. Remove the lamb and set aside.

4 Add the onion, garlic and ginger paste to the pan and cook for 1–2 minutes, stirring continuously. Stir in the ground spices and cook for 1 minute. Return the meat to the pan with any meat juices that have seeped out while it has been standing. Add the cayenne, stock and seasoning.

5 Bring to a boil, cover and simmer for 30 minutes or until the lamb is tender. Stir in the rice, then cover and cook for another 15 minutes. Add the lemon juice and coconut milk and simmer for another 2 minutes.

6 Ladle the soup into six warmed bowls and garnish with sprigs of cilantro and lightly toasted shredded coconut.

fiery tomato soup
with red bell pepper cream

This dazzling soup can be made as fiery or as mild as you want by increasing or reducing the number of chiles.

you will need

3–3½ pounds plum tomatoes, halved

5 red chiles, seeded

1 red bell pepper, halved and seeded

2 red onions, roughly chopped

6 garlic cloves, crushed

2 tablespoons sun-dried tomato paste

3 tablespoons olive oil

1⅔ cups vegetable stock

salt and ground black pepper

wild arugula leaves, to garnish

FOR THE BELL PEPPER CREAM

1 red bell pepper, halved and seeded

2 teaspoons olive oil

½ cup crème frâiche

few drops of Tabasco

Serves 4

3 Roast with the mixed vegetables for 30–40 minutes, until blistered.

4 Transfer the pepper for the pepper cream to a bowl as soon as it is cooked. Cover with plastic wrap and let cool. Peel off the skin and purée the flesh in a food processor or blender with half the crème fraîche. Pour into a bowl and stir in the remaining crème frâiche. Season and add a dash of Tabasco. Chill until needed.

5 Process the roasted vegetables in batches, adding a ladleful of stock to each batch to make a smooth, thick purée. Depending on how juicy the tomatoes are, you may not need all the stock.

1 Preheat the oven to 400°F. Place the tomatoes, chiles, red pepper, onions, garlic and tomato paste in a roasting pan. Toss all the vegetables, drizzle with the oil and toss again, then roast for 40 minutes, until tender and the pepper skin is slightly charred.

2 Meanwhile make the pepper cream. Lay the red pepper halves skin-side up on a baking sheet and brush with the olive oil.

6 Press the purée through a sieve into a saucepan and stir in more stock if you want to thin the soup. Heat the soup gently and season it well. Ladle the soup into bowls and spoon red pepper cream into the center of each portion. Pile wild arugula leaves on top to garnish.

cook's tip

The pepper cream is a bit runny when first processed, but it firms up when chilled.

goan potato soup
with spiced pea samosas

you will need

¼ cup sunflower oil

2 teaspoons black mustard seeds

1 large onion, chopped

1 red chile, seeded and chopped

½ teaspoon ground turmeric

¼ teaspoon cayenne pepper

2 pounds potatoes, cut into cubes

4 fresh curry leaves

3 cups water

8 ounces spinach leaves, torn if large

1⅔ cups coconut milk

handful of cilantro leaves

salt and ground black pepper

FOR THE SAMOSA DOUGH

2½ cups all-purpose flour

¼ teaspoon salt

2 tablespoons sunflower oil

⅔ cup warm water

FOR THE SAMOSA FILLING

¼ cup sunflower oil

1 small onion, finely chopped

1½ cups frozen peas, thawed

1 tablespoon grated fresh ginger root

1 green chile, seeded and finely chopped

3 tablespoons water

12 ounces cooked potatoes, finely diced

1½ teaspoons ground coriander

1 teaspoon garam masala

1½ teaspoons ground cumin

¼ teaspoon cayenne pepper

2 teaspoons lemon juice

2 tablespoons chopped cilantro

vegetable oil, for deep-frying

Serves 4

In Goa this soup would be served as a complete meal. Both soup and samosas are simple to prepare, and make a substantial vegetarian lunch.

1 Make the samosa dough. Mix the flour and salt in a bowl and make a well in the middle. Add the oil and water and mix in the flour to make a soft dough. Knead briefly on a lightly floured surface. Wrap in plastic wrap and chill for 30 minutes.

2 To make the filling, heat the oil in a frying pan and add the onion. Cook for 6–7 minutes, until golden. Add the peas, ginger, chile and water. Cover and simmer for 5–6 minutes, until the peas are cooked. Add the potatoes, spices and lemon juice. Cook over low heat for 2–3 minutes, then stir in the chopped cilantro. Season well and let cool.

3 Divide the dough into eight pieces. On a floured surface, roll out one piece into a 7-inch round. Keep the remaining dough covered. Cut the round in half and place 2 tablespoons of the filling on each half toward one corner. Dampen the edges and fold the dough over the filling. Pinch the edges together to seal and form triangles. Repeat with the remaining dough and filling.

4 Heat the oil for deep-frying to 375°F, or until a cube of bread rises and sizzles in 30 seconds. Fry the samosas for 4–5 minutes, turning once. Drain on paper towels.

5 To make the soup, heat the oil in a large pan. Add the mustard seeds, cover and cook until they begin to pop. Add the onion and chili and cook for 5–6 minutes, until softened.

6 Stir in the turmeric, cayenne, potatoes, curry leaves and water. Cover and cook over low heat for 15 minutes, stirring occasionally, until the potatoes are tender. Add the spinach and cook for 5 minutes. Stir in the coconut milk and cook for another 5 minutes. Season and add the cilantro leaves before ladling the soup into bowls. Serve with the vegetable samosas.

spiced red lentil soup
with parsley cream

Crispy shallots and a parsley cream top this rich soup, which is inspired by the dhals of Indian cooking. Chunks of bacon add texture.

1 Heat a frying pan and add the cumin and coriander seeds. Roast them over high heat for a few seconds, shaking the pan until they smell aromatic. Transfer to a mortar and crush using a pestle. Mix in the turmeric; set aside.

2 Heat the oil in a large saucepan. Add the onion and garlic and cook for 4–5 minutes, until softened. Add the spice mixture and cook for 2 minutes, stirring continuously.

3 Place the bacon in the pan and pour in the stock. Bring to a boil, cover and simmer gently for 30 minutes.

4 Add the red lentils and cook for 20 minutes or until the lentils and ham hock are tender. Stir in the tomatoes and cook for another 5 minutes.

5 Remove the bacon from the pan and set it aside until cool enough to handle. Let the soup cool slightly, then process in a food processor or blender until almost smooth. You may have to do this in batches. Return the soup to the rinsed-out pan. Cut the meat from the hock, discarding skin and fat, then stir it into the soup and reheat.

6 Heat the vegetable oil in a frying pan and fry the shallots for 10 minutes, until crisp and golden. Remove from the pan using a draining spoon and drain on paper towels.

7 To make the parsley cream, stir the chopped parsley into the yogurt and season well. Ladle the soup into bowls and add a dollop of the parsley cream to each. Pile some crisp shallots onto each portion and serve immediately.

you will need

1 teaspoon cumin seeds

½ teaspoon coriander seeds

1 teaspoon ground turmeric

2 tablespoons olive oil

1 onion, chopped

2 garlic cloves, chopped

1 smoked ham hock

5 cups vegetable stock

1¼ cups red lentils

14-ounce can chopped tomatoes

1 tablespoon vegetable oil

3 shallots, thinly sliced

FOR THE PARSLEY CREAM

3 tablespoons chopped fresh parsley

⅔ cup plain yogurt

salt and ground black pepper

Serves 6

tagine-style lamb soup with butternut squash

you will need

2 tablespoons olive oil

1 pound lamb fillet, trimmed and cut into small cubes

1 large onion, chopped

2 garlic cloves, crushed

2 celery stalks, diced

1 tablespoon harissa

2 teaspoons all-purpose flour

5 cups hot vegetable stock

14-ounce can chopped tomatoes

⅓ cup dried apricots

2-pound butternut squash, seeded, peeled and cut into small cubes

salt and ground black pepper

FOR THE MINTED COUSCOUS

1¼ cups vegetable stock

1 cup couscous

2 tomatoes, peeled, seeded and diced

2 tablespoons chopped fresh mint

Serves 6

A tagine is a stew that takes its name from the cone-shaped pot in which it is traditionally cooked. This soup is inspired by the tagines of Morocco.

1 Heat the oil in a heavy saucepan. Add the lamb and cook for 5 minutes or until browned all over. Use a draining spoon to remove the lamb from the pan and set it aside.

2 Add the onion and garlic to the fat remaining in the pan and cook for 4–5 minutes, until softened. Add the celery, cover and cook gently for 5 minutes to soften slightly. Stir in the harissa and flour, and cook for 2 minutes. Gradually whisk in the hot vegetable stock.

3 Stir in the tomatoes and apricots and bring to a boil. Cover and simmer gently for 20 minutes. Season well.

4 Add the cubes of butternut squash and return the lamb to the soup. Cover and cook for about 25 more minutes, stirring occasionally, until both lamb and squash are tender.

5 Meanwhile, prepare the couscous. Pour the vegetable stock into a large saucepan and bring to a boil. Stir in the couscous and cook for about 1 minute, then remove the pan from heat, cover and let stand for 5 minutes. Then mix the chopped tomatoes and mint into the couscous with a fork.

6 Ladle the soup into warmed bowls and pile a spoonful of couscous into the center. Serve immediately, with extra harissa on the side.

cook's tip

Harissa is a hot and spicy condiment, based on a paste of chiles. It is added to stews and other dishes during cooking, and can also be served as an accompaniment for those who want to pep up the flavor at the table.

pad thai
red monkfish soup

This light and creamy coconut soup provides a base for a colorful fusion
of red-curried monkfish and pad Thai, the classic stir-fried noodle dish of Thailand.

1 Soak the noodles in boiling water for 10 minutes, or according to the package instructions. Drain.

2 Heat the oil in a wok or saucepan over high heat. Add the garlic and cook for 2 minutes. Stir in the curry paste and cook for 1 minute.

3 Add the monkfish and stir-fry over high heat for 4–5 minutes, until just tender. Pour in the coconut cream and stock. Stir in the fish sauce and sugar, and bring just to a boil. Add the drained noodles and cook for 1–2 minutes, until tender.

4 Stir in half the peanuts, half the scallions, half the bean sprouts, the basil and seasoning. Ladle the soup into deep bowls and sprinkle the remaining peanuts. Garnish with the remaining scallions, bean sprouts and the red chile.

you will need

6 ounces flat rice noodles

2 tablespoons vegetable oil

2 garlic cloves, chopped

1 tablespoon red curry paste

1 pound monkfish tail, cut into bite-size pieces

1¼ cups coconut milk

3 cups hot chicken stock

3 tablespoons Thai fish sauce (*nam pla*)

1 tablespoon sugar

4 tablespoons roughly chopped roasted peanuts

4 scallions, shredded lengthwise

2 ounces bean sprouts

large handful of fresh Thai basil leaves

salt and ground black pepper

1 red chile, seeded and cut lengthwise into slivers, to garnish

Serves 4

corn and red chili chowder

Corn and chiles make good bedfellows, and here the cool combination of creamed corn and milk is the perfect foil for the raging heat of the chiles.

1 Process the tomatoes and onion in a food processor or blender to a smooth purée. Add the creamed corn and process again, then set aside. Preheat the broiler to high.

2 Put the peppers, skin-sides up, on a broiler pan and brush with oil. Broil for 8–10 minutes, until the skins blacken and blister. Transfer to a bowl and cover with plastic wrap, then let cool. Peel and dice the peppers, then set them aside.

3 Heat the oil in a large saucepan and add the chopped chiles and garlic. Cook, stirring, for 2–3 minutes, until softened.

4 Add the ground cumin and coriander, and cook for another minute. Stir in the corn purée and cook for about 8 minutes, stirring occasionally.

5 Pour in the milk and stock, then stir in the corn kernels, potatoes, red pepper and seasoning to taste. Cook for 15–20 minutes, until the corn and potatoes are tender.

6 Pour into deep bowls and add the cream, then sprinkle on the chopped parsley and serve immediately.

you will need

2 tomatoes, skinned

1 onion, roughly chopped

13-ounce can creamed corn

2 red bell peppers, halved and seeded

1 tablespoon olive oil, plus extra for brushing

3 red chiles, seeded and chopped

2 garlic cloves, chopped

1 teaspoon ground cumin

1 teaspoon ground coriander

2½ cups milk

1½ cups chicken stock

3 ears of corn, kernels removed

1 pound potatoes, finely diced

4 tablespoons heavy cream

4 tablespoons chopped fresh parsley

salt and ground black pepper

Serves 6

red bean soup
with guacamole salsa

you will need

2 tablespoons olive oil

2 onions, chopped

2 garlic cloves, chopped

2 teaspoons ground cumin

¼ teaspoon cayenne pepper

1 tablespoon paprika

1 tablespoon tomato paste

½ teaspoon dried oregano

14-ounce can chopped tomatoes

2 14-ounce cans red kidney beans,
drained and rinsed

3¾ cups water

salt and ground black pepper

Tabasco, to serve

FOR THE GUACAMOLE SALSA

2 avocados

1 small red onion, finely chopped

1 green chile, seeded and finely chopped

1 tablespoon chopped cilantro

juice of 1 lime

Serves 6

This soup is in Tex-Mex style and it is served with a cooling avocado and lime salsa. If you relish chiles, add a little more cayenne for a truly fiery experience.

1 Heat the oil in a large, heavy saucepan and add the onions and garlic. Cook for 4–5 minutes, until softened. Add the cumin, cayenne and paprika, and cook for 1 minute, stirring continuously.

2 Stir in the tomato paste and cook for a few seconds, then stir in the oregano. Add the chopped tomatoes, kidney beans and water.

3 Bring the tomato and bean mixture to a boil and simmer for 15–20 minutes. Cool the soup slightly, then purée it in a food processor or blender until smooth. Return to the rinsed-out saucepan and add seasoning to taste.

4 To make the guacamole salsa, halve, pit and peel the avocados, then dice them finely. Place in a small bowl and gently, but thoroughly, mix with the finely chopped red onion and chile, and the cilantro and lime juice.

5 Reheat the soup and ladle into bowls. Spoon a little guacamole salsa into the middle of each and serve, offering Tabasco for those who want to spice up their soup.

rich and smooth

These soups, inspired by classic French cuisine, are perfect for easy and elegant entertaining. They include a few of the finer things in life: duck is paired with blueberries, scallops with caviar, and salmon with a ruby salsa.

cream of mushroom soup with goat cheese crostini

Classic cream of mushroom soup is still a favorite, especially with the addition of luxuriously crisp and garlicky croûtes.

1 Melt the butter in a pan and cook the onion and garlic for 5 minutes. Add the mushrooms, cover and cook for 10 minutes, stirring occasionally.

2 Stir in the flour and cook for 1 minute. Stir in the sherry and stock and bring to a boil, then simmer for 15 minutes. Cool slightly, then purée it in a food processor or blender until smooth.

3 Meanwhile, prepare the crostini. Heat the oil in a small pan. Add the shallot and button mushrooms, and cook for 8–10 minutes, until softened. Drain well and transfer to a food processor. Add the parsley and process until finely chopped.

4 Preheat the broiler. Brush the brown cap mushrooms with oil and broil for 5–6 minutes.

5 Toast the slices of baguette, rub with the garlic and put a spoonful of cheese on each. Top each grilled mushroom with some mushroom mixture and place on the crostini.

6 Return the soup to the pan and stir in the cream. Season, then reheat gently. Ladle the soup into six bowls. Float a crostini in the center of each and garnish with chervil.

you will need

2 tablespoons butter

1 onion, chopped

1 garlic clove, chopped

6 cups chestnut or brown cap mushrooms, roughly chopped

1 tablespoon all-purpose flour

3 tablespoons dry sherry

3¾ cups vegetable stock

⅔ cup heavy cream

salt and ground black pepper

fresh chervil sprigs, to garnish

FOR THE CROSTINI

1 tablespoon olive oil, plus extra for brushing

1 shallot, chopped

1½ cups button mushrooms, finely chopped

1 tablespoon chopped fresh parsley

6 brown cap mushrooms

6 slices baguette

1 small garlic clove

1 cup soft goat cheese

Serves 6

butternut squash and blue cheese risotto soup

This is, in fact, a very wet risotto, but it bears more than a passing resemblance to soup and makes a very elegant first course for a dinner party.

1 Place the butter in a large saucepan with the oil and heat gently. Add the onions and celery, and cook for 4–5 minutes, until softened. Stir in the butternut squash and cook for another 3–4 minutes, then add the sage.

2 Add the rice and cook for 1–2 minutes, stirring, until the grains are slightly translucent. Add the chicken stock a ladleful at a time.

3 Cook until each ladleful of stock has been absorbed before adding the next. Continue adding the stock in this way until you have a very wet rice mixture. Season and stir in the cream.

4 Meanwhile, heat the oil in a frying pan and fry the sage leaves for a few seconds until crisp. Drain. Stir the blue cheese into the risotto soup and ladle into bowls. Garnish with the fried sage leaves.

you will need

2 tablespoons butter

2 tablespoons olive oil

2 onions, finely chopped

½ celery stalk, finely sliced

1 small butternut squash, peeled, seeded and cut into small cubes

1 tablespoon chopped sage

1½ cups risotto or arborio rice

5 cups hot chicken stock

2 tablespoons heavy cream

4 ounces blue cheese, finely diced

salt and ground black pepper

2 tablespoons olive oil

4 large sage leaves, to garnish

salt and ground black pepper

Serves 4

salmon soup
with ruby salsa and rouille

This fish soup is the perfect choice for summer entertaining. Sorrel is a good partner for salmon, but dill or fennel are equally delicious alternatives.

you will need

6 tablespoons olive oil

1 onion, chopped

1 leek, chopped

1 celery stalk, chopped

1 fennel bulb, roughly chopped

1 red bell pepper, seeded and sliced

3 garlic cloves, chopped

grated zest and juice of 2 oranges

1 bay leaf

14-ounce can chopped tomatoes

5 cups fish stock

pinch of cayenne pepper

1¾ pounds salmon fillet, skinned

1¼ cups heavy cream

salt and ground black pepper

4 thin slices baguette, to serve

FOR THE RUBY SALSA

2 tomatoes, peeled, seeded and diced

½ small red onion, very finely chopped

1 tablespoon cod's roe

1 tablespoon chopped fresh sorrel

FOR THE ROUILLE

½ cup mayonnaise

1 garlic clove, crushed

1 teaspoon sun-dried tomato paste

Serves 4

1 Heat the oil in a large saucepan and add the onion, leek, celery, fennel, pepper and garlic. Cover and cook gently for 20 minutes or until all the vegetables are softened.

2 Add the orange zest and juice, bay leaf and tomatoes. Cover and cook for 4–5 minutes, stirring occasionally. Add the stock and cayenne, cover the pan and simmer for 30 minutes.

3 Add the salmon and cook gently for 8–10 minutes, until just cooked. Use a draining spoon to remove the salmon.

4 Flake the salmon into large pieces, discard bones, and set aside.

5 Meanwhile, mix all the prepared salsa ingredients in a bowl and then set aside.

6 To make the rouille, mix the mayonnaise with the crushed garlic and the sun-dried tomato paste. Toast the baguette slices on both sides and set aside.

7 Let the soup cool slightly, then purée it in a food processor or blender until smooth, and press it through a fine sieve into the rinsed-out saucepan. Stir in the heavy cream and season well. Add the flaked salmon and reheat the soup gently without letting it boil.

8 Ladle the soup into bowls and float the toasted baguette slices on top. Add a spoonful of rouille to each slice of baguette and spoon some ruby salsa on top. Serve immediately.

cook's tip

For a smart presentation, choose wide, shallow soup plates, so that the rouille-topped toast sits on top of the pieces of flaked salmon.

cream of duck soup
with blueberry relish

you will need

2 duck breasts

4 strips of bacon, chopped

1 onion, chopped

1 garlic clove, chopped

2 carrots, diced

2 celery stalks, chopped

4 large open mushrooms, chopped

1 tablespoon tomato paste

2 duck legs, chopped into pieces

1 tablespoon all-purpose flour

3 tablespoons brandy

⅔ cup port

1¼ cups red wine

3¾ cups chicken stock

1 bay leaf

2 sprigs fresh thyme

1 tablespoon red currant jelly

⅔ cup heavy cream

salt and ground black pepper

FOR THE BLUEBERRY RELISH

1¼ cups blueberries

1 tablespoon sugar

grated zest and juice of 2 limes

1 tablespoon chopped fresh parsley

1 tablespoon balsamic vinegar

Serves 4

This delicious, rich soup is ideal for smart autumnal occasions. You can use a whole duck, but cooking with duck breasts and legs is easier.

1 Use a sharp knife to score the skin and fat on the duck breasts. Preheat a heavy pan. Place the duck breasts in the pan, skin-sides down, and cook for 8–10 minutes, until golden. Turn and cook for another 5–6 minutes, until tender.

2 Remove the duck from the pan and set aside. Drain off some of the duck fat, leaving about 3 tablespoons in the pan.

3 Add the bacon, onion, garlic, carrots, celery and mushrooms to the pan and cook for 10 minutes, stirring occasionally. Stir in the tomato paste and cook for 2 minutes. Remove the skin and bones from the duck legs and chop the flesh. Add to the pan and cook for 5 minutes.

4 Stir in the flour and cook for 1 minute. Gradually stir in the brandy, port, wine and stock and bring to a boil, stirring. Add the bay leaf, thyme and red currant jelly, then stir until the jelly melts. Reduce the heat and simmer for 1 hour.

5 Meanwhile, make the relish. Put the blueberries, sugar, lime zest and juice, parsley and vinegar in a small bowl. Very lightly bruise the blueberries with a fork, leaving some of the berries whole. Set aside until required.

6 Strain the soup through a colander, then press it through a fine sieve into a clean saucepan. Bring to a boil, reduce the heat and simmer gently for 10 minutes.

7 Meanwhile, remove and discard the skin and fat from the duck breasts and cut the meat into thin strips. Add the meat strips to the soup with the heavy cream and season well. Bring just to the boiling point.

8 Ladle the soup into warmed bowls and top each serving with a dollop of the blueberry relish. Serve piping hot.

vermouth soup with seared scallops, arugula oil and caviar

Seared scallops form an elegant tower in the center of this *crème de la crème* of fine soups. The caviar garnish looks—and tastes—superb.

1 Prepare the arugula oil first. Process the arugula leaves and olive oil in a food processor or blender for 1–2 minutes to give a green paste. Line a small bowl with a piece of muslin and scrape the paste into it. Gather up the muslin and squeeze it well to extract the green, arugula-flavored oil from the paste. Set aside.

2 Melt the butter in a large saucepan. Add the shallots and cook over low heat for 8–10 minutes, until soft but not browned. Add the wine and vermouth and boil for 8–10 minutes, until reduced to about a quarter of the volume.

3 Add the stock and bring back to a boil. Boil until reduced by half. Pour in the heavy and light creams, and return to a boil. Reduce the heat and simmer for 12–15 minutes, until just thick enough to coat the back of a spoon.

4 Strain the soup through a fine sieve into the rinsed-out pan, and set aside.

5 Heat a ridged griddle or frying pan. Brush the scallops with oil, add them to the pan and sear for 1–2 minutes on each side, until just cooked, when they will be white and tender.

6 Reheat the soup gently, then taste and season. Arrange three scallops, one on top of the other, in the center of each of four warmed, shallow soup plates. Ladle the hot soup around the scallops and top them with a little of the caviar. Drizzle some arugula oil on the surface of the soup, then sprinkle with snipped chives.

you will need

2 tablespoons butter

5 shallots, sliced

1¼ cups dry white wine

1¼ cups good-quality vermouth

3¾ cups fish stock

1¼ cups heavy cream

1¼ cups light cream

1 tablespoon olive oil

12 large scallops

salt and ground black pepper

1 tablespoon caviar and snipped chives, to garnish

FOR THE ARUGULA OIL

4 ounces arugula leaves

½ cup olive oil

Serves 4

you will need

2 tablespoons sunflower oil

1 onion, chopped

3 pears, peeled, cored and chopped

1⅔ cups vegetable stock

½ teaspoon paprika

juice of ½ lemon

6 ounces Roquefort cheese

salt and ground black pepper

watercress sprigs, to garnish

FOR THE CARAMELIZED PEARS

¼ cup butter

2 pears, halved, cored and cut into wedges

Serves 4

pear and roquefort soup
with caramelized pears

Like most fruit-based soups, this is served in small portions. It makes an unusual and seasonal appetizer for an autumn dinner party.

1 Heat the oil in a saucepan. Add the onion and cook for 4–5 minutes, until soft. Add the pears and stock, then bring to a boil. Cook for 8–10 minutes, until the pears are very soft. Stir in the paprika, lemon juice, cheese and seasoning.

2 Cool the soup slightly, then purée it in a food processor until smooth, then pass it through a fine sieve. Return the soup to the pan.

3 To make the caramelized pears, melt the butter in a frying pan and add the pears. Cook for 8–10 minutes, turning occasionally, until golden and beginning to caramelize.

4 Reheat the soup gently, then ladle into small, shallow bowls and add a few caramelized pear wedges to each portion. Garnish with tiny sprigs of watercress and serve immediately.

creamy eggplant soup
with mozzarella and gremolata

Gremolata, a classic Italian mixture of garlic, lemon and parsley, adds a flourish of fresh flavor to this rich cream soup.

1 Heat the oil in a large saucepan and add the shallots and garlic. Cook for 4–5 minutes, until softened. Add the eggplant and cook for about 25 minutes, stirring occasionally, until they are very soft and browned.

2 Pour in the chicken stock and cook for about 5 minutes. Let the soup cool slightly.

3 Purée the soup in a food processor or blender until smooth. Return to the rinsed-out saucepan, season. Add the cream and parsley, and bring to a boil.

4 Mix the ingredients for the gremolata. Ladle the soup into bowls and lay the mozzarella on top. Sprinkle with gremolata and serve.

you will need

2 tablespoons olive oil

2 shallots, chopped

2 garlic cloves, chopped

2¼ pounds eggplant, trimmed and roughly chopped

4 cups chicken stock

⅔ cup heavy cream

2 tablespoons chopped fresh parsley

6 ounces buffalo mozzarella, thinly sliced

salt and ground black pepper

FOR THE GREMOLATA

2 garlic cloves, finely chopped

grated zest of 2 lemons

1 tablespoon chopped fresh parsley

Serves 6

potato and fennel soup
with warm rosemary scones

The simple flavors in this fine soup are enhanced by the delicate perfume of herb flowers, and complemented by rosemary-seasoned scones.

1 Melt the butter in a pan. Add the onions and cook gently for 10 minutes, stirring occasionally, until very soft. Add the fennel seeds and cook for 2–3 minutes. Stir in the fennel and potatoes.

2 Cover the vegetables with a sheet of wet waxed paper and put a lid on the pan. Cook gently for 10 minutes until very soft.

3 Remove the paper. Pour in the stock, bring to a boil, cover and simmer for 35 minutes.

4 Meanwhile, make the scones. Preheat the oven to 450°F and grease a baking sheet. Sift the flour, salt and baking powder into a bowl. Stir in the rosemary, then rub in the butter. Add the milk and mix to form a soft dough.

you will need

6 tablespoons butter
2 onions, chopped
1 teaspoon fennel seeds, crushed
3 bulbs fennel, coarsely chopped
2 pounds potatoes, thinly sliced
5 cups chicken stock
⅔ cup heavy cream
salt and ground black pepper
handful of fresh herb flowers and
1 tablespoon snipped fresh chives,
to garnish

FOR THE ROSEMARY SCONES
2 cups self-rising flour
½ teaspoon salt
1 teaspoon baking powder
2 teaspoons chopped fresh rosemary
¼ cup butter
⅔ cup milk
1 egg, beaten, to glaze

Serves 4

5 Knead very lightly on a floured surface. Roll out to ¾ inch thick. Stamp out 12 rounds with a cutter. Brush with the egg and bake on the prepared baking sheet for 8–10 minutes, until risen and golden. Cool on a wire rack until warm.

6 Let the soup cool slightly, then purée it in a food processor or blender until smooth. Press through a sieve into the rinsed-out saucepan. Stir in the cream with seasoning to taste. Reheat gently but do not boil.

7 Ladle the soup into four warmed soup bowls and sprinkle a few herb flowers and snipped chives on each. Serve immediately with the warm rosemary scones.

cappuccino of puy lentils, lobster and tarragon

Adding ice-cold butter a little at a time is the secret of whipping up the good froth that gives the clever cappuccino effect on this soup.

1 Bring a large saucepan of water to a boil. Lower the live lobster into the water and cover the pan. Cook for 15–20 minutes, then drain the lobster and let cool.

2 Put the lentils in a pan and cover with cold water. Add the vegetables, garlic and herbs. Bring to a boil and simmer for 20 minutes.

3 Drain the lentils and discard the vegetables and herbs. Purée the lentils in a food processor or blender until smooth. Set aside.

4 Break the claws off the lobster, crack them open and remove the meat from inside. Break off the tail, split it open and remove the meat. Cut all the meat into bite-size pieces.

5 Pour the fish stock into a large clean saucepan and bring to a boil. Lightly stir in the lentil purée and cream, but do not mix too much at this point, otherwise you will not be able to create the cappuccino effect. The mixture should still be quite watery in places. Season well.

6 Using either a hand-held blender or electric beater, whisk up the soup mixture, adding the butter one piece at a time, until it is very frothy.

7 Divide the lobster meat among the bowls and carefully pour in the soup. Garnish with sprigs of tarragon and serve immediately.

you will need

1–1½-pound live lobster
⅔ cup Puy lentils
1 carrot, halved
1 celery stalk, halved
1 small onion, halved
1 garlic clove
1 bay leaf
large bunch of tarragon, tied firmly
4 cups fish stock
½ cup heavy cream
2 tablespoons butter, finely diced and chilled until ice cold
salt and ground black pepper
fresh tarragon sprigs, to garnish

Serves 6

asparagus and pea soup
with parmesan cheese

This bright and tasty soup uses every inch of the asparagus, including the woody ends which are used for making the stock.

1 Cut the woody ends from the asparagus, then set the spears aside. Roughly chop the woody ends and place them in a large saucepan. Cut off and chop the green parts of the leeks and add to the asparagus stalks with the bay leaf, carrot, celery, parsley stems and the cold water. Bring to a boil and simmer for 30 minutes. Strain the stock and discard the vegetables.

2 Cut the tips off the asparagus and set aside, then cut the stems into short pieces. Chop the remainder of the leeks.

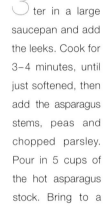

3 Melt the butter in a large saucepan and add the leeks. Cook for 3–4 minutes, until just softened, then add the asparagus stems, peas and chopped parsley. Pour in 5 cups of the hot asparagus stock. Bring to a boil, reduce the heat and cook for 6–8 minutes, until all the vegetables are tender. Season well.

4 Cool the soup slightly, then purée it in a food processor or blender until smooth. Press the purée through a very fine sieve into the rinsed-out saucepan. Stir in the cream and lemon zest.

5 Bring a small saucepan of water to a boil and cook the asparagus tips for 2–3 minutes, until just tender. Drain and refresh under cold water. Reheat the soup, but do not let it boil.

6 Ladle the soup into six warmed bowls and garnish with the asparagus tips. Serve immediately, with shavings of Parmesan cheese and plenty of ground black pepper.

you will need

12 ounces asparagus

2 leeks

1 bay leaf

1 carrot, roughly chopped

1 celery stalk, chopped

few stems of fresh parsley

7½ cups cold water

2 tablespoons butter

5 ounces fresh garden peas

1 tablespoon chopped fresh parsley

½ cup heavy cream

grated zest of ½ lemon

salt and ground black pepper

shavings of Parmesan cheese, to serve

Serves 6

roasted pumpkin soup
with pumpkin crisps

The pumpkin is roasted whole, then split open and scooped out to make this delicious soup; topped with crisp strips of fried pumpkin, it is a real treat.

1 Preheat the oven to 400°F. Prick the pumpkin around the top several times with a fork. Brush the pumpkin with plenty of the oil and bake for 45 minutes or until tender. Let sit until cool enough to handle.

2 Take care when cutting the pumpkin, as there may still be a lot of hot steam inside. When cool enough to handle, scoop out and discard the seeds. Scoop out and chop the flesh.

3 Heat about 4 tablespoons of the remaining oil (you may not have to use all of it) in a large saucepan and add the onions, garlic and ginger, then cook gently for 4–5 minutes. Add the coriander, turmeric and cayenne, and cook for 2 minutes. Stir in the pumpkin flesh and stock. Bring to a boil, reduce the heat and simmer for 20 minutes.

4 Cool the soup slightly, then purée it in a food processor or blender until smooth. Return the soup to the rinsed-out saucepan and season well.

5 Meanwhile, prepare the pumpkin crisps. Using a swivel-blade potato peeler, pare long thin strips off the wedge of pumpkin. Heat the oil in a small saucepan and fry the strips in batches for 2–3 minutes, until crisp. Drain on paper towels.

6 Reheat the soup and ladle it into bowls. Top with the pumpkin crisps and garnish each portion with sesame seeds and cilantro leaves.

cook's tip

If only very large pumpkins are available, simply cut off two or three large wedges weighing 3–3½ pounds in total. Brush them with oil and roast as above for 20–30 minutes or until tender.

you will need

3–3½-pound pumpkin
6 tablespoons olive oil
2 onions, chopped
3 garlic cloves, chopped
3-inch piece fresh ginger root, grated
1 teaspoon ground coriander
½ teaspoon ground turmeric
pinch of cayenne pepper
4 cups vegetable stock
salt and freshly ground black pepper
1 tablespoon sesame seeds and
cilantro leaves, to garnish

FOR THE PUMPKIN CRISPS

wedge of fresh pumpkin, seeded
½ cup olive oil

Serves 6–8

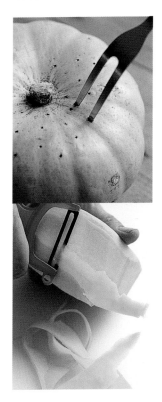

lunch in a bowl

Take inspiration from casseroles and stews, pasta dishes and roasts, and let soup take center stage as the main event of the meal. These robust soups are full of flavor—perfect for people with big appetites.

cod, fava bean and spinach
chowder with crisp croutons

Fresh cod and vegetables are abundant in this thick and creamy soup, which is finished with crisp whole-grain croutons to soak up the delicious liquid.

1 Pour the milk and cream into a large saucepan and bring to a boil. Add the cod and bring back to a boil. Reduce the heat and simmer for 2–3 minutes, then remove from heat and let stand for about 6 minutes, until the fish is just cooked. Use a slotted spoon to remove the fish from the cooking liquid.

you will need

4 cups milk

⅔ cup heavy cream

1½ pounds cod fillet, skinned and boned

3 tablespoons olive oil

1 onion, sliced

2 garlic cloves, finely chopped

1 pound potatoes, thickly sliced

1 pound fresh fava beans, podded

8 ounces baby spinach leaves

pinch of grated nutmeg

2 tablespoons snipped fresh chives

salt and ground black pepper

fresh chives, to garnish

FOR THE CROUTONS

¼ cup olive oil

6 slices whole-grain bread, crusts removed and cut into large cubes

Serves 6

2 Using a fork, flake the cooked cod into chunky pieces, removing any bones or skin, then cover and set aside.

3 Heat the olive oil in a large saucepan and add the onion and garlic. Cook for about 5 minutes, until softened, stirring occasionally. Add the potatoes, stir in the milk mixture and bring to a boil. Reduce the heat and cover the pan. Cook for 10 minutes. Add the fava beans; cook for 10 more minutes or until the beans are tender and the potatoes just begin to break up.

4 Meanwhile, to make the croutons, heat the oil in a frying pan and add the bread cubes. Cook over medium heat, stirring often, until golden all over. Remove using a draining spoon and let drain on paper towels.

5 Add the cod to the soup and heat through gently. Just before serving, add the spinach and stir for 1–2 minutes, until wilted. Season the soup well and stir in the nutmeg and chives.

6 Ladle the soup into six warmed soup bowls and pile the croutons on top. Garnish with fresh chives and serve immediately.

cook's tip

When fresh fava beans are out of season, frozen beans are acceptable. Cook them for the time recommended on the package.

wild mushroom soup
with soft polenta

This rich soup, served with soft Parmesan-enriched polenta, provides plenty of scope for individual variations, depending on your choice of wild mushrooms.

1 Put the porcini in a bowl and pour in the hot water. Let them soak for about 30 minutes. Drain, then strain the liquid through a fine sieve; reserve both the liquid and the mushrooms.

2 Melt the butter in a large saucepan. Add the onion and garlic and cook for 4–5 minutes, until softened. Add the mixed wild mushrooms and cook for another 3–4 minutes.

3 Add the dried mushrooms and strain in the soaking liquid through a muslin-lined sieve or coffee filter. Pour in the wine and stock, and cook for 15 minutes or until reduced by half. Remove from heat and cool slightly.

4 Ladle half the soup into a food processor or blender and process until almost smooth. Pour the processed soup back into the soup remaining in the saucepan and set aside.

5 To make the polenta, bring the milk to a boil and pour in the polenta in a steady stream, stirring continuously. Cook for about 5 minutes or until the polenta begins to come away from the side of the pan. Beat in the butter, then stir in the Parmesan.

6 Return the soup to the heat and bring just to a boil. Stir in the whole-grain mustard and season well. Divide the polenta among six bowls and ladle the soup around it. Sprinkle on grated Parmesan and chopped parsley.

cook's tip

Many large supermarkets now sell a range of wild and cultivated mushrooms. If you can't find any, then substitute a mixture of well-flavored cultivated varieties such as shiitake and chestnut.

you will need

scant ½ cup dried porcini mushrooms

¾ cup hot water

¼ cup butter

1 large red onion, chopped

3 garlic cloves, chopped

1¾ cups mixed wild mushrooms, trimmed

½ cup light red wine

5 cups vegetable stock

½ teaspoon whole-grain mustard

salt and ground black pepper

chopped fresh parsley, to garnish

FOR THE POLENTA

3 cups milk

1 cup quick-cook polenta

¼ cup butter

⅔ cup freshly grated Parmesan cheese, plus extra to serve

Serves 6

southern succotash soup
with chicken

Based on a vegetable dish from the southern states, this soup includes succulent fresh corn kernels, which give it a richness that complements the chicken.

1 Bring the chicken stock to a boil in a large saucepan. Add the chicken breasts and bring back to a boil. Reduce the heat and cook for 12–15 minutes, until cooked through and tender. Use a draining spoon to remove the chicken from the pan and let cool. Reserve the stock.

2 Melt the butter in a saucepan. Add the onions and cook for 4–5 minutes, until softened.

3 Add the bacon and cook for 5–6 minutes, until beginning to brown. Sprinkle in the flour and cook for 1 minute, stirring continuously. Gradually stir in the hot stock and bring to a boil, stirring until thickened. Remove from heat.

4 Stir in the corn and half the milk. Return to the heat and cook, stirring occasionally, for 12–15 minutes, until the corn is tender.

5 Cut the chicken into bite-size pieces and stir into the soup. Stir in the lima beans and the remaining milk. Bring to a boil and cook for 5 minutes, season well and stir in the parsley.

you will need

3 cups chicken stock

4 boneless, skinless chicken breasts

¼ cup butter

2 onions, chopped

4 ounces bacon, chopped

¼ cup all-purpose flour

4 ears of corn, kernels removed

1¼ cups milk

14-ounce can lima beans, drained

3 tablespoons chopped fresh parsley

salt and ground black pepper

Serves 4

variation

Canned corn can be used instead of fresh corn.

soup of toulouse sausage
with borlotti beans and bread crumbs

A hearty soup, this recipe is based loosely on cassoulet. French sausages and Italian beans contribute flavor and substance, and the soup is topped with golden bread crumbs.

1 Place the beans in a saucepan. Cover with plenty of cold water and bring to a boil, then boil for 10 minutes. Drain well.

2 Heat a large saucepan and dry-fry the pancetta until browned and the fat runs. Add the sausages and cook for 4–5 minutes, stirring occasionally, until beginning to brown. Add the onion and garlic and cook for 3–4 minutes, until softened. Add the beans, carrots, leeks, tomatoes and tomato paste, then add the stock. Stir, bring to a boil and cover.

3 Simmer for about 1¼ hours or until the beans are tender, then stir in the kale and cook for 12–15 more minutes. Season well.

4 Meanwhile, melt the butter in a frying pan and fry the bread crumbs for 4–5 minutes, stirring until golden, then stir in the Parmesan.

5 Ladle the soup into six bowls. Sprinkle the fried bread crumb mixture on each, then serve.

you will need

generous 1¼ cups borlotti beans, soaked overnight and drained

4-ounce piece pancetta, finely chopped

6 Toulouse sausages, thickly sliced

1 large onion, finely chopped

2 garlic cloves, chopped

2 carrots, finely diced

2 leeks, finely chopped

6 tomatoes, peeled, seeded and chopped

2 tablespoons tomato paste

5⅔ cups vegetable stock

6 ounces kale, roughly shredded

2 tablespoons butter

2 cups fresh white bread crumbs

⅔ cup freshly grated Parmesan cheese

salt and ground black pepper

Serves 6

meatballs in a pasta soup
with fresh basil

you will need

14-ounce can cannellini beans, drained and rinsed

4 cups vegetable stock

3 tablespoons olive oil

1 onion, finely chopped

2 garlic cloves, chopped

1 small red chile, seeded and finely chopped

2 celery stalks, finely chopped

1 carrot, finely chopped

1 tablespoon tomato paste

11 ounces small pasta shapes

large handful of fresh basil, torn

salt and ground black pepper

basil leaves, to garnish

freshly grated Parmesan cheese, to serve

FOR THE MEATBALLS

1 thick slice white bread, crusts removed

¼ cup milk

12 ounces lean ground beef or veal

2 tablespoons chopped fresh parsley

grated zest of 1 orange

2 garlic cloves, crushed

1 egg, beaten

2 tablespoons olive oil

Serves 4

These meatballs are delicious—scented with orange and garlic, they are served in a rustic pasta soup, which is thickened with puréed beans.

1 First prepare the meatballs. Break the bread into small pieces and place them in a bowl. Add the milk and let soak for about 10 minutes. Add the ground beef or veal, parsley, orange zest and garlic, and season well. Mix well with your hands.

2 When the bread is thoroughly incorporated with the meat, add enough beaten egg to bind the mixture. Shape small spoonfuls of the mixture into balls about the size of a large olive.

3 Heat the oil in a frying pan and fry the meatballs in batches for 6–8 minutes, until browned all over. Use a draining spoon to remove them from the pan and set aside.

4 Purée the cannellini beans with a little of the vegetable stock in a food processor or blender until smooth. Set aside.

5 Heat the olive oil in a large saucepan. Add the chopped onion and garlic, chile, celery and carrot, and cook for 4–5 minutes. Cover and cook gently for another 5 minutes, then stir in the tomato paste, the bean purée and the remaining vegetable stock. Bring the soup to a boil and cook for about 10 minutes.

6 Stir in the pasta shapes and simmer for 8–10 minutes, until the pasta is tender but not soft. Add the meatballs and basil and cook for another 5 minutes. Season the soup well before ladling it into warmed bowls. Garnish each bowl of soup with a basil leaf, and serve with freshly grated Parmesan cheese.

cook's tip

Choose hollow pasta shapes for this soup, which will scoop up the soup as you eat. Look for small and medium-size pasta shapes that are made especially for soup.

roast vegetable medley
with sun-dried tomato bread

Winter meets summer in this soup recipe. Serve it with bread baked with a hint of added summer flavor in the form of sun-dried tomatoes.

1 Preheat the oven to 400°F. Cut the thick ends of the parsnip quarters into four pieces, then place them in a large roasting pan. Add the onions, carrots, leeks, rutabaga and potatoes, and spread them in an even layer.

2 Drizzle the olive oil onto the vegetables. Add the thyme and unpeeled garlic cloves. Toss well and roast for 45 minutes, until all the vegetables are tender and slightly charred.

3 Meanwhile, to make the sun-dried tomato bread, cut diagonal slits along the loaf, taking care not to cut right through it. Mix the butter with the garlic, sun-dried tomatoes and parsley. Spread the mixture into each slit, then press the bread back together. Wrap the loaf in aluminum foil and bake for 15 minutes; open the foil for the last 4–5 minutes. Discard the thyme from the roasted vegetables. Squeeze the garlic cloves from their skins onto the vegetables.

4 Process about half the vegetables with the stock in a food processor or blender until almost smooth. Pour into a pan and add the remaining vegetables. Bring to a boil and season well. Ladle the soup into bowls and garnish with fresh thyme leaves. Serve the hot bread with the soup.

you will need

4 parsnips, quartered lengthwise

2 red onions, cut into thin wedges

4 carrots, thickly sliced

2 leeks, thickly sliced

1 small rutabaga, cut into bite-size pieces

4 potatoes, cut into chunks

¼ cup olive oil

few sprigs of fresh thyme

1 bulb garlic, broken into cloves, unpeeled

4 cups vegetable stock

salt and ground black pepper

fresh thyme sprigs, to garnish

FOR THE SUN-DRIED
TOMATO BREAD

I ciabatta loaf (about 10 ounces)

6 tablespoons butter, softened

1 garlic clove, crushed

4 sun-dried tomatoes, finely chopped

2 tablespoons chopped fresh parsley

Serves 4

roast lamb shanks
in pearl barley broth

Succulent roasted lamb shanks studded with garlic and rosemary make a fabulous meal when served in a hearty vegetable, barley and tomato broth.

1 Preheat the oven to 300°F. Make small cuts all over the lamb and insert slivers of garlic and sprigs of rosemary into them.

2 Heat the oil in a flameproof casserole and brown the shanks two at a time. Remove and set aside. Add the carrots, celery and onion in batches and cook until lightly browned. Put all the vegetables in the casserole with the bay leaf and thyme. Pour in stock to cover, place the lamb shanks on top and roast for 2 hours.

3 Meanwhile, pour the remaining stock into a large saucepan. Add the pearl barley, then bring to a boil. Reduce the heat, cover and simmer for 1 hour or until the barley is tender.

4 Remove the lamb shanks from the casserole using a slotted spoon.

5 Skim the fat from the surface of the roasted vegetables, then add them to the broth. Stir in the tomatoes, lemon zest and parsley.

you will need

4 small lamb shanks
4 garlic cloves, cut into slivers
handful of small fresh rosemary sprigs
2 tablespoons olive oil
2 carrots, diced
2 celery stalks, diced
1 large onion, chopped
1 bay leaf
few sprigs of fresh thyme
5 cups lamb stock
2 ounces pearl barley
1 pound tomatoes, peeled and chopped
grated zest of 1 large lemon
2 tablespoons chopped fresh parsley
salt and ground black pepper

Serves 4

6 Bring the soup back to a boil. Reduce the heat and simmer for 5 minutes. Add the lamb shanks and heat through, then season. Put a lamb shank into each of four large bowls, then ladle the barley broth onto the meat and serve immediately.

mexican mixed bean chili
with monterey jack nachos

Steaming bowls of beef chili, packed with beans, are delicious topped with crushed tortillas and cheese. Pop the bowls under the broiler to melt the cheese, if desired.

1 Heat the oil in a large saucepan over high heat and brown the meat all over until golden. Use a draining spoon to remove it from the pan. Reduce the heat and add the onions, garlic and chiles, then cook for 4–5 minutes, until softened.

2 Add the chili powder and ground cumin, and cook for another 2 minutes. Return the meat to the pan, then stir in the bay leaves, tomato paste and beef stock. Bring to a boil.

3 Reduce the heat, cover and simmer for about 45 minutes or until the meat is tender.

4 Put a quarter of the beans into a bowl and mash with a potato masher. Stir these into the soup to thicken it slightly. Add the remaining beans and simmer for 5 minutes. Season and stir in the chopped cilantro. Ladle the soup into bowls and spoon tortilla chips on top. Pile grated cheese on the tortilla chips and serve.

you will need

3 tablespoons olive oil

12 ounces rump steak, cut into small cubes

2 onions, chopped

2 garlic cloves, crushed

2 green chiles, seeded and chopped

2 tablespoons mild chili powder

1 teaspoon ground cumin

2 bay leaves

2 tablespoons tomato paste

3¾ cups beef stock

2 14-ounce cans mixed beans,
drained and rinsed

3 tablespoons chopped cilantro

salt and ground black pepper

FOR THE TOPPING

bag of plain tortilla chips, lightly crushed

2 cups Monterey Jack
cheese, grated

Serves 4

variation

Use Cheddar cheese instead of Monterey Jack, if you prefer.

celeriac soup
with cabbage, bacon and herbs

Versatile, yet often overlooked, celeriac is a winter vegetable that makes excellent soup. It tastes wonderful topped with a complementary seasonal version of a salsa.

you will need

¼ cup butter

2 onions, chopped

1½ pounds celeriac, roughly diced

1 pound potatoes, roughly diced

5 cups vegetable stock

⅔ cup light cream

salt and ground black pepper

sprigs of fresh thyme, to garnish

FOR THE CABBAGE AND BACON TOPPING

1 small savoy cabbage

¼ cup butter

6 ounces bacon, roughly chopped

1 tablespoon roughly chopped fresh thyme

1 tablespoon roughly chopped fresh rosemary

Serves 4

1 Melt the butter in a saucepan. Add the onions and cook for 4–5 minutes, until softened. Add the celeriac. Cover the vegetables with a wet piece of waxed paper, then put a lid on the pan and cook gently for 10 minutes.

2 Remove the paper and stir in the potatoes and stock. Bring to a boil, reduce the heat and simmer for 20 minutes or until the vegetables are very tender. Let cool slightly. Using a draining spoon, remove about half the celeriac and potatoes from the soup and set them aside.

3 Purée the soup in a food processor or blender. Return the soup to the rinsed-out pan with the reserved celeriac and potatoes.

4 Prepare the cabbage and bacon mixture. Discard the tough outer leaves from the cabbage. Roughly tear the remaining leaves, discarding any hard stalks, and blanch them in boiling salted water for 2–3 minutes. Refresh under cold running water and drain.

5 Melt the butter in a large frying pan and cook the bacon for 3–4 minutes. Add the cabbage, thyme and rosemary, and stir-fry for 5–6 minutes, until tender. Season well.

6 Add the cream to the soup and season it well, then reheat gently until piping hot. Ladle the soup into bowls and pile the cabbage mixture in the center of each portion. Garnish with sprigs of fresh thyme.

braised cabbage soup
with beef and horseradish cream

This delicious winter soup really is a complete main course in a bowl. Cook the beef as rare or as well-done as desired.

you will need

2 pounds red cabbage, hard core discarded and leaves finely shredded

2 onions, finely sliced

1 large apple, peeled, cored and chopped

3 tablespoons brown sugar

2 garlic cloves, crushed

¼ teaspoon grated nutmeg

½ teaspoon caraway seeds

3 tablespoons red wine vinegar

4 cups beef stock

1½ pounds sirloin

2 tablespoons olive oil

salt and ground black pepper

watercress, to garnish

FOR THE HORSERADISH CREAM

1–2 tablespoons grated fresh horseradish

2 teaspoons wine vinegar

½ teaspoon Dijon mustard

⅔ cup heavy cream

Serves 6

1 Preheat the oven to 300°F. Combine the red cabbage with the onions, apple, brown sugar, garlic, nutmeg, caraway seeds, red wine vinegar and 3 tablespoons of the stock. Add plenty of seasoning, then put into a large buttered casserole and cover with a tight-fitting lid. Bake for 2½ hours, checking every 30 minutes or so to ensure that the cabbage is not becoming too dry. If necessary, add a few more tablespoons of the stock. Remove the casserole from the oven and set aside. Increase the oven temperature to 450°F.

2 Trim off most of the fat from the sirloin, leaving a thin layer. Tie the meat with string. Heat the oil in a heavy frying pan until smoking hot. Add the beef and cook on all sides until well browned.

3 Transfer to a roasting pan and roast for 15–20 minutes for medium-rare or 25–30 minutes for well-done beef.

4 To make the horseradish cream, mix the grated horseradish, wine vinegar, mustard and seasoning with 3 tablespoons of the cream. Lightly whip the remaining cream and fold in the horseradish mixture. Chill until needed.

5 Spoon the braised cabbage into a large saucepan and pour in the remaining stock. Bring just to the boiling point.

6 Remove the beef from the oven and let rest for 5 minutes, then remove the string and carve into slices. Ladle the soup into bowls and divide the beef among them, resting on the cabbage. Spoon a little horseradish cream onto each serving of beef, and garnish with small bunches of watercress. Serve immediately.

irish country soup

Traditionally, buttered chunks of brown bread, or Irish soda bread, would be served with this hearty one-pot meal based on the classic Irish stew.

1 Heat the oil in a large saucepan, add the lamb in batches and cook, turning occasionally until well browned all over. Use a slotted spoon to remove the lamb from the pan and set aside.

2 When all the lamb has been cooked, add the onions to the pan and cook for 4–5 minutes, until the onions are browned. Return the meat to the pan and add the leeks. Pour in the water, then bring to a boil. Reduce the heat, then cover and simmer gently for about 1 hour.

3 Add the potatoes, carrots and thyme, and continue cooking for another 40 minutes, until the lamb is tender. Remove from heat and let stand for 5 minutes to let the fat settle on the surface of the soup.

4 Use a large spoon or ladle to skim off the fat. Carefully pour off the stock from the soup into a clean saucepan and whisk the butter into it. Stir in the parsley and season well, then pour the liquid back over the soup ingredients.

5 Ladle the soup into warmed bowls and garnish with sprigs of fresh thyme. Serve with chunks of brown or Irish soda bread.

variation

The vegetables in this rustic soup can be varied according to the season. Rutabaga, turnip, celeriac and even cabbage could be added in place of some of the listed vegetables.

you will need

1 tablespoon vegetable oil

1½ pounds boneless lamb chops, trimmed and cut into small cubes

2 small onions, quartered

2 leeks, thickly sliced

4 cups water

2 large potatoes, cut into chunks

2 carrots, thickly sliced

sprig of fresh thyme, plus extra to garnish

1 tablespoon butter

2 tablespoons chopped fresh parsley

salt and ground black pepper

brown or Irish soda bread, to serve

Serves 4

ribollita

This is a classic rustic soup from the Tuscan region in Italy. For an authentic version you should use cavolo nero cabbage, which is available at larger supermarkets.

you will need

generous ½ cup cannellini beans,
soaked overnight and drained

8 garlic cloves, unpeeled

2 tablespoons olive oil

6 celery stalks, chopped

3 carrots, chopped

2 onions, chopped

14-ounce can plum tomatoes, drained

2 tablespoons chopped fresh flat-leaf parsley

grated zest and juice of 1 lemon

1¾ pounds cavolo nero cabbage, sliced

1 day-old ciabatta loaf

salt and ground black pepper

olive oil, to serve

Serves 4

1 Put the beans in a saucepan and cover with fresh water. Bring to a boil and boil for 10 minutes. Drain again. Cover generously with fresh cold water and add six garlic cloves. Bring to a boil, cover and simmer for 45–60 minutes, until the beans are tender. (The cooking time varies according to how old the beans are.) Set the beans aside in their cooking liquid.

2 Heat the oil in a saucepan. Peel and chop the remaining garlic and add it to the pan with the celery, carrots and onions. Cook gently for 10 minutes, until beginning to soften.

3 Stir in the tomatoes, parsley, lemon zest and juice. Cover and simmer for 25 minutes. Add the sliced cavolo nero cabbage and half the cannellini beans with enough of their cooking liquid to cover all of the ingredients. Simmer for 30 minutes.

4 Meanwhile, process the remaining beans with a little of their remaining cooking liquid in a food processor or blender until just smooth. Add to the pan and pour in boiling water to thin the mixture to the consistency of a thick soup.

5 Remove the crust from the ciabatta and tear the bread into rough pieces, then stir them into the soup. Season well. This soup should be very thick, but you may need to add a little more boiling water, as the consistency varies depending on the bread. Ladle the soup into bowls and drizzle on a little olive oil. Serve immediately.

cauliflower and broccoli soup
with cheddar cheese croûtes

Creamy cauliflower soup is given real bite by adding chunky cauliflower and broccoli florets and crusty bread piled high with melting Cheddar cheese.

1 Melt the butter in a large saucepan and add the onion and garlic. Cook for 4–5 minutes, until softened. Add about half the cauliflower and all the potato. Pour in the chicken stock and bring to a boil. Reduce the heat and simmer for 20 minutes, until very soft.

2 Meanwhile, cook the rest of the cauliflower in boiling salted water for about 6 minutes, or until just tender. Use a draining spoon to remove the the florets and refresh under cold running water, then drain well.

3 Add the broccoli to the boiling salted water and cook for 3–4 minutes, until just tender. Drain and refresh under cold water, then drain well. Add to the cauliflower and set aside.

4 Cool the soup slightly, then process it in a food processor or blender until smooth. Return the soup to the rinsed-out saucepan. Add the cream and salt and pepper to taste, then heat gently until piping hot. Add the blanched cauliflower and broccoli and heat through.

5 Meanwhile, preheat the broiler to high. Broil the bacon until very crisp, then let cool slightly. Ladle the soup into flameproof bowls.

6 Tear the baguette into four ragged pieces and place one in the center of each bowl. Sprinkle grated cheese on the bread and stand the bowls on one or two baking sheets. Broil for 2–3 minutes, until the cheese is melted and bubbling. Take care when serving the hot bowls.

7 Roughly chop the bacon and sprinkle it on the melted cheese, then sprinkle the parsley on top and serve immediately.

you will need

¼ cup butter

1 onion, chopped

1 garlic clove, chopped

2 cauliflowers, broken into florets

1 large potato, cut into chunks

3¾ cups chicken stock

8 ounces broccoli, broken into florets

⅔ cup light cream

6 strips bacon

1 small baguette

2 cups aged grated Cheddar cheese

salt and ground black pepper

roughly chopped fresh parsley, to garnish

Serves 4

soups of the sun

Inspired by the sun-drenched coast of the Mediterranean and warm Caribbean shores, these recipes draw on flavorful produce, from sun-kissed olives and oranges to fish and shellfish.

saffron-flavored mussel soup

There's a fragrant taste of the sea from the Spanish coast in this creamy soup filled with the jet black shells of plump mussels.

1 Scrub the mussels and pull off the beards. Put into a large saucepan with the wine and parsley stems. Cover, bring to a boil and cook for 4–5 minutes, shaking the pan occasionally, until the mussels have opened. Discard the stems and any mussels that refuse to open.

2 Drain the mussels over a large bowl, reserving the cooking liquid. When cool enough to handle, remove about half of the cooked mussels from their shells. Set aside with the remaining mussels in their shells.

3 Melt the butter in a large saucepan and add the leeks, celery, carrot and garlic, and cook for 5 minutes, until softened. Strain the reserved mussel cooking liquid through a fine sieve or muslin. Add to the pan and cook over high heat for 8–10 minutes to reduce slightly. Strain into a clean saucepan, add the saffron threads and cook for 1 minute.

you will need

3–3½ pounds fresh mussels

2½ cups white wine

few fresh parsley stems

¼ cup butter

2 leeks, finely chopped

2 celery stalks, finely chopped

1 carrot, chopped

2 garlic cloves, chopped

large pinch of saffron threads

2½ cups heavy cream

3 tomatoes, peeled, seeded and chopped

salt and ground black pepper

2 tablespoons chopped fresh chives, to garnish

Serves 4

4 Add the cream and bring back to a boil. Season well. Add all the mussels and the tomatoes and heat gently to warm through. Ladle the soup into four bowls, then sprinkle on the chopped chives and serve immediately.

tomato, ciabatta and basil oil soup

Throughout Europe, bread is a popular ingredient for thickening soup, and this recipe shows how wonderfully quick and easy this method can be.

1 To make the basil oil, process the basil leaves and oil in a food processor or blender for 1–2 minutes to make a paste. Line a small bowl with muslin and scrape the paste into it. Gather up the muslin and squeeze it firmly around the paste to extract all the basil-flavored oil. Set aside.

2 Heat the oil in a large saucepan and cook the onion and garlic for 4–5 minutes, until softened.

3 Add the wine, water, fresh and canned tomatoes. Bring to a boil, reduce the heat and cover the pan, then simmer for 3–4 minutes. Add the sugar and season well. Stir in the bread.

4 Ladle the soup into bowls. Garnish with basil and drizzle the basil oil on each portion.

you will need

3 tablespoons olive oil

1 red onion, chopped

6 garlic cloves, chopped

1¼ cups white wine

⅔ cup water

12 plum tomatoes, quartered

2 14-ounce cans plum tomatoes

½ teaspoon sugar

½ ciabatta loaf, broken into bite-size pieces

salt and ground black pepper

basil leaves, to garnish

FOR THE BASIL OIL

4 ounces basil leaves

½ cup olive oil

Serves 4

artichoke soup with
anchoke and artichoke bruschetta

Jerusalem artichokes originate from North America, yet lend themselves beautifully to the methods and flavors of Mediterranean cooking.

1 Prepare a large bowl of cold water with a squeeze of lemon juice added. Peel and dice the Jerusalem artichokes, adding them to the water as soon as each one is prepared. This will prevent them from discoloring.

2 Melt the butter in a large, heavy saucepan. Drain the artichokes and add to the pan with the potatoes, onion, garlic, celery and fennel. Stir well and cook for 10 minutes, stirring occasionally, until beginning to soften.

3 Pour in the stock and bring to a boil, then simmer for 10–15 minutes, until all the vegetables are softened. Cool the soup slightly, then process in a food processor or blender until smooth. Press it through a sieve into a clean pan. Add the cream and nutmeg, and season well.

4 To make the bruschetta, lightly toast the French bread slices on both sides. Rub each slice with the garlic clove and set aside. Melt the butter in a small saucepan. Add the artichoke hearts and cook for 3–4 minutes, turning once.

5 Spread the tapenade on the toast and arrange pieces of artichoke heart on top. Top with anchovy fillets and garnish with basil leaves.

6 Reheat the artichoke soup without letting it boil, then ladle it into shallow bowls. Serve the bruschetta with the soup.

cook's tip

Look for artichoke hearts that have been bottled in flavored olive oil rather than brine—they have a superior flavor.

you will need

squeeze of lemon juice

1 pound Jerusalem artichokes

5 tablespoons butter

6 ounces potatoes, roughly diced

1 small onion, chopped

1 garlic clove, chopped

1 celery stalk, chopped

1 small bulb fennel, halved, cored and chopped

5 cups vegetable stock

1¼ cups heavy cream

pinch of freshly grated nutmeg

salt and ground black pepper

basil leaves, to garnish

FOR THE ARTICHOKE AND ANCHOVY BRUSCHETTA

6 thick slices French bread

1 garlic clove

¼ cup unsalted butter

14-ounce can artichoke hearts, drained and halved

3 tablespoons tapenade

9 salted anchovy fillets, halved lengthwise

Serves 6

bourride of red snapper
and fennel with black olives

you will need

1½ tablespoons olive oil

1 onion, chopped

3 garlic cloves, chopped

2 fennel bulbs, halved, cored and thinly sliced

4 tomatoes, chopped

1 bay leaf

1 sprig fresh thyme

5 cups fish stock

1½ pounds red snapper, scaled and filleted

8 slices baguette

1 garlic clove

2 tablespoons sun-dried tomato paste

12 black olives, pitted and quartered

salt and ground black pepper

fresh fennel fronds, to garnish

FOR THE MAYONNAISE

2 egg yolks

2 teaspoons white wine vinegar

1¼ cups extra virgin olive oil

Serves 4

This fish soup from Provence in France is made with fresh mayonnaise. The secret of success is to cook the soup gently.

1 Heat the olive oil in a large, heavy saucepan. Add the chopped onion and garlic and cook for 5 minutes, until softened. Add the fennel and cook for another 2–3 minutes. Stir in the tomatoes, bay leaf, thyme and fish stock.

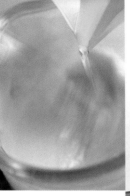

2 Bring the mixture to a boil, then reduce the heat and simmer for 30 minutes.

3 Meanwhile, make the mayonnaise. Put the egg yolks and vinegar in a bowl. Season and whisk well. Whisk in the oil, a little at a time. As the mayonnaise begins to emulsify and thicken, increase the speed with which you add the oil, from a few drops at a time to a slow trickle. Transfer to a large bowl and set aside.

4 Cut each snapper fillet into two or three pieces, then add them to the soup and cook gently for 5 minutes. Use a draining spoon to remove the snapper and set aside.

5 Strain the cooking liquid through a fine sieve, pressing the vegetables with a ladle to extract as much flavor as possible. Whisk about a ladleful of the soup into the mayonnaise, then whisk in the remaining soup all at once.

6 Return the soup to a clean saucepan and cook very gently, whisking continuously, until the mixture is very slightly thickened. Add the snapper to the soup and set it aside.

7 Toast the baguette slices on both sides. Rub each slice with the clove of garlic and spread with sun-dried tomato paste. Divide the olives among the toasted bread slices.

8 Very gently reheat the soup, but do not let it boil, then ladle it into bowls. Top each portion with two toasts and garnish with fennel.

roasted eggplant and zucchini
soup with tzatziki

A fusion of flavors from the sunny Greek islands creates this fabulous soup, which is served with tzatziki, the popular combination of cucumber and creamy yogurt.

1 Preheat the oven to 400°F. Place the eggplant and zucchini in a roasting pan. Add the onion and garlic, drizzle on the olive oil and spread out the vegetables in an even layer. Roast for 35 minutes, turning once, until tender and slightly charred.

2 To make the tzatziki, place the cucumber in a colander and sprinkle with the salt. Place on a plate or bowl and let sit for 30 minutes.

3 Mix the garlic with the vinegar and stir into the yogurt. Pat the cucumber dry on paper towels and fold it into the yogurt. Season to taste and stir in the mint. Chill until needed.

4 Place half the roasted vegetables in a food processor or blender. Add the stock and process until almost smooth. (You may have to do this in batches.) Then pour into a large saucepan and add the remaining vegetables.

5 Bring the soup slowly to a boil and season well. Stir in the chopped oregano.

6 Ladle the soup into four bowls. Garnish with mint sprigs and serve immediately. Pass the bowl of tzatziki so that your guests can add a dollop or two to their soup.

you will need

2 large eggplant, roughly diced

4 large zucchini, roughly diced

1 onion, roughly chopped

4 garlic cloves, roughly chopped

3 tablespoons olive oil

5 cups vegetable stock

1 tablespoon chopped fresh oregano

salt and ground black pepper

mint sprigs, to garnish

FOR THE TZATZIKI

1 cucumber, peeled, seeded and diced

2 teaspoons salt

2 garlic cloves, crushed

1 teaspoon white wine vinegar

1 cup plain yogurt

small bunch of fresh mint leaves, chopped

Serves 4

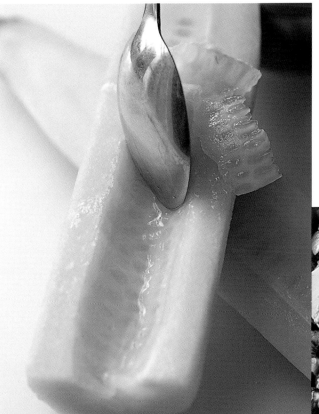

caribbean salt cod and okra soup with creamed yams

Inspired by the ingredients of the Caribbean, this colorful chunky soup is served in deep bowls around chive-flavored creamed yams.

1 Drain and skin the salt cod, then rinse it under cold running water. Cut the flesh into bite-size pieces, removing any bones, and set aside.

2 Heat the oil in a heavy saucepan. Add the garlic, onion and chile, and cook for 4–5 minutes, until softened. Add the salt cod and cook for 3–4 minutes, until it begins to color. Stir in the tomatoes, wine and bay leaves and bring to a boil. Pour in the water, bring to a boil, reduce the heat and simmer for 10 minutes.

3 Meanwhile, trim the stalk ends off the okra and cut the pods into chunks. Add to the soup and cook for 10 minutes. Stir in the callaloo or spinach and cook for 5 minutes, until the okra is tender.

4 Meanwhile, prepare the creamed yams. Peel the yams and cut into large dice, then place in a saucepan with the lemon juice and add cold water to cover. Bring to a boil and cook for 15–20 minutes, until tender. Drain well, then return the yams to the pan and dry out over the heat for a few seconds. Mash with the butter and cream, and season well. Stir in the chives.

5 Season the soup and stir in the chopped parsley. Spoon portions of creamed yams into the centers of six soup bowls and ladle the soup around it. Serve immediately.

you will need

7 ounces salt cod, soaked for 24 hours, changing the water several times
1 tablespoon olive oil
1 garlic clove, chopped
1 onion, chopped
1 green chile, seeded and chopped
6 plum tomatoes, peeled and chopped
1 cup white wine
2 bay leaves
3¾ cups water
8 ounces okra
8 ounces callaloo or spinach
2 tablespoons chopped fresh parsley
salt and ground black pepper

FOR THE CREAMED YAMS
1½ pounds yams
juice of 1 lemon
¼ cup butter
2 tablespoons heavy cream
1 tablespoon snipped fresh chives

Serves 6

cook's tip

Callaloo is a Caribbean leafy vegetable similar in flavor to spinach, but with smaller, more pointed leaves. Both spinach or Swiss chard are suitable alternatives. If you can't find fresh yams, make the dish using sweet potatoes instead.

soft-shell crab, shrimp and corn gumbo

A well-flavored chicken and shellfish stock gives this dish the authentic taste of a traditional Louisiana gumbo. Serve with spoons and forks to eat the corn.

1 To make the stock, peel the shrimp and put the shells into a pan. Set the shrimp aside. Add the remaining ingredients to the pan. Bring to a boil and skim. Cover and cook for 1 hour.

2 To make the gumbo, heat the oil in a large pan, add the onion and garlic and cook for 3–4 minutes. Add the bacon and cook for 3 minutes. Stir in the flour and cook for 3–4 minutes.

3 When the mixture is turning golden, strain in the stock, stirring continuously. Add the celery, pepper, chile and tomatoes, bring to a boil and simmer for 5 minutes. Cut the corn into 1-inch slices, and add to the gumbo.

4 To prepare the crabs, use scissors to cut off the eyes and mouth, then cut across the face and push your fingers into the opening to hook out the stomach, a jelly-like sac. Turn the crab over and pull off the little tail flap. Lift up both sides of the shell and pull out the gills or "dead man's fingers." Quarter the crabs, then add to the gumbo with the shrimp.

5 Simmer for 15 minutes, until the crabs and corn are cooked. Season, then stir in the parsley and scallions. Serve in deep bowls.

you will need

2 tablespoons vegetable oil

1 onion, chopped

1 garlic clove, chopped

4 ounces bacon, chopped

⅓ cup all-purpose flour

1 celery stalk, chopped

1 red bell pepper, seeded and chopped

1 red chile, seeded and chopped

1 pound plum tomatoes, chopped

2 large ears of corn

4 soft-shell crabs, washed well

2 tablespoons chopped fresh parsley

small bunch of scallions, roughly chopped

salt and ground black pepper

FOR THE STOCK

12 ounces whole uncooked shrimp

2 large chicken wings

1 carrot, thickly sliced

3 celery stalks, sliced

1 onion, sliced

handful of parsley stems

2 bay leaves

6¼ cups water

Serves 6

moroccan chicken soup
with charmoula butter

This memorable soup, inspired by the ingredients of North Africa, is spiced with chili and served with a rich and pungent lemon butter creamed with crisp bread crumbs.

1 Melt the butter in a large, heavy saucepan. Add the chicken strips and cook for 5–6 minutes, until beginning to brown. Use a draining spoon to remove it from the pan and set aside. Add the onion and garlic and cook over low heat for 4–5 minutes, until softened.

2 Stir in the flour and cook for 3–4 minutes, stirring, until beginning to brown. Stir in the harissa and cook for another minute. Gradually pour in the stock and cook for 2–3 minutes, until slightly thickened. Stir in the tomatoes.

3 Return the chicken to the soup and add the chickpeas. Cover and cook over low heat for 20 minutes. Season well.

4 Meanwhile, to make the charmoula, put the butter into a bowl and beat in the cilantro, garlic, cumin, chile, saffron threads, lemon zest and paprika. When the mixture is well combined, stir in the coarse bread crumbs.

5 Ladle the soup into warmed bowls. Spoon a little of the charmoula into the center of each and let sit for a few seconds to let the butter melt into the soup before serving with lemon wedges.

you will need

¼ cup butter

1 pound chicken breasts, cut into strips

1 onion, chopped

2 garlic cloves, crushed

1½ teaspoons all-purpose flour

1 tablespoon harissa

4 cups chicken stock

14-ounce can chopped tomatoes

14-ounce can chickpeas, drained and rinsed

salt and ground black pepper

lemon wedges, to serve

FOR THE CHARMOULA

¼ cup slightly salted butter, at room temperature

2 tablespoons chopped cilantro

2 garlic cloves, crushed

1 teaspoon ground cumin

1 red chile, seeded and chopped

pinch of saffron threads

finely grated zest of ½ lemon

1 teaspoon paprika

1 cup dried bread crumbs

Serves 6

light and healthy

Homemade soups are full of good things to eat, but we can be heavy-handed with rich ingredients such as cream. These flavorful broths and soups, packed with fresh vegetables and fish, are healthier options.

noodle, bok choy
and seared salmon ramen

Ramen is a Japanese noodle soup for which a good stock is essential. Here, the lightly spiced broth is enhanced by slices of fresh salmon and crisp vegetables.

1 Pour the stock into a large saucepan and add the ginger, garlic, and a third of the scallions. Add the soy sauce and sake. Bring to a boil, then reduce the heat; simmer for 30 minutes.

2 Meanwhile, remove any pin bones from the salmon using tweezers, then cut the salmon on the slant into 12 slices, using a very sharp knife.

3 Brush a ridged griddle or frying pan with the oil and heat until very hot. Sear the salmon slices for 1–2 minutes on each side, until tender and marked by the ridges of the pan. Set aside.

4 Cook the ramen or udon noodles in boiling water for 4–5 minutes or according to the package instructions. Drain well and refresh under cold running water. Drain again and set aside.

5 Strain the broth into a clean pan and season to taste, then bring to a boil. Break the bok choy into leaves and add to the pan. Using a fork, twist the noodles into four nests and put these into deep bowls. Add three slices of salmon to each bowl. Divide the remaining scallions, the chile and bean sprouts among the bowls, then ladle the steaming broth around the ingredients.

you will need

6¼ cups good vegetable stock

1-inch piece fresh ginger root, finely sliced

2 garlic cloves, crushed

6 scallions, sliced

3 tablespoons soy sauce

3 tablespoons sake

1 pound salmon fillet, skinned and boned

1 teaspoon peanut oil

12 ounces ramen or udon noodles

4 small heads bok choy

1 red chile, seeded and sliced

¼ cup bean sprouts

salt and ground black pepper

Serves 4

tom yam gung with tofu

One of the most refreshing and healthy soups, this fragrant dish is a famous Thai specialty, which would make an ideal light lunch or supper.

3 Strain the stock into a clean saucepan. Stir in the remaining chile, the shiitaki mushrooms, scallions, fish sauce, lime juice and sugar. Simmer for 3 minutes. Add the fried tofu and heat through for 1 minute. Mix in the chopped cilantro and season to taste. Serve immediately in warmed bowls.

cook's tip

Fresh kaffir limes and leaves are available at Southeast Asian stores. If you cannot find them, use freeze-dried leaves, which are widely available, or ordinary lime zest.

you will need

2 tablespoons peanut oil

11 ounces firm tofu, cut into small bite-size pieces

5 cups good vegetable stock

1 tablespoon Thai chili jam (*nam pick pow*)

grated zest of 1 kaffir lime

1 shallot, finely sliced

1 garlic clove, finely chopped

2 kaffir lime leaves, shredded

3 red chiles, seeded and shredded

1 lemongrass stalk, finely chopped

6 shiitaki mushrooms, thinly sliced

4 scallions, shredded

3 tablespoons Thai fish sauce (*nam pla*)

3 tablespoons lime juice

1 teaspoon sugar

3 tablespoons chopped cilantro

salt and ground black pepper

Serves 4

1 Heat the oil in a wok and fry the tofu for 4–5 minutes, until golden, turning occasionally. Use a draining spoon to remove it and set aside. Transfer the oil from the wok into a large, heavy saucepan.

2 Add the stock, chili jam, kaffir lime zest, shallot, garlic, lime leaves, two-thirds of the chiles and the lemongrass to the saucepan. Bring to a boil and simmer for 20 minutes.

lemon and pumpkin
moules marinière

Based on the classic French shellfish dish, this mussel soup is thickened and flavored with fresh pumpkin.

you will need

2¼ pounds fresh mussels

1¼ cups dry white wine

1 large lemon

1 bay leaf

1 tablespoon olive oil

1 onion, chopped

1 garlic clove, crushed

1½ pounds pumpkin or squash, seeded, peeled and roughly chopped

3¾ cups vegetable stock

2 tablespoons chopped fresh dill

salt and ground black pepper

lemon wedges, to serve

Serves 4

1 Scrub the mussels in cold water and pull off the dark hairy beards protruding from the shells. Discard any open mussels that do not shut when tapped sharply, and put the rest into a large saucepan. Pour in the white wine.

2 Pare large pieces of zest from the lemon and squeeze the juice, then add both to the mussels with the bay leaf. Cover and bring to a boil, then cook for 4–5 minutes, shaking the pan occasionally, until all the mussels have opened. Drain the mussels in a colander over a large bowl. Reserve the cooking liquid and the mussels.

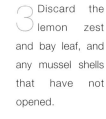

3 Discard the lemon zest and bay leaf, and any mussel shells that have not opened.

4 When all the mussels are cool enough to handle, set aside

a few in their shells for the garnish. Remove the remaining mussels from their shells. Strain the reserved cooking liquid through a muslin-lined sieve to remove any sand or grit.

5 Heat the oil in a large, clean saucepan. Add the onion and garlic and cook for 4–5 minutes, until softened. Add the pumpkin flesh and the strained mussel cooking liquid. Bring to a boil and simmer, uncovered, for 5–6 minutes. Pour in the vegetable stock and cook for another 25–30 minutes, until the pumpkin has almost disintegrated.

6 Cool the soup slightly, then process it in a food processor or blender until smooth. Return the soup to the rinsed-out saucepan and season well. Stir in the chopped dill and the shelled mussels, then bring just to a boil.

7 Ladle the soup into warmed soup plates and garnish with the reserved mussels in their shells. Serve lemon wedges with the soup.

summer herb soup
with grilled radicchio

The sweetness of shallots and leeks in this soup is balanced beautifully by the slightly acidic sorrel with its hint of lemon, and a bouquet of summer herbs.

1 Put the wine, shallots and garlic into a heavy saucepan and bring to a boil. Cook for 2–3 minutes, until softened. Add the leeks, potato and zucchini with enough of the water to come about halfway up the vegetables. Lay a wet piece of waxed paper over the vegetables and put a lid on the pan, then cook gently for 10–15 minutes, until softened. Remove the paper and add the fresh herbs and lettuce. Cook for 1–2 minutes or until wilted.

2 Pour in the remaining water and vegetable stock and simmer for 10–12 minutes. Cool the soup slightly, then process it in a food processor or blender until smooth. Return the soup to the rinsed-out saucepan and season well.

3 Cut the radicchio into thin wedges that hold together, then brush the cut-sides with the oil. Heat a ridged griddle or frying pan until very hot and add the radicchio wedges.

you will need

2 tablespoons dry white wine

2 shallots, finely chopped

1 garlic clove, crushed

2 leeks, sliced

1 large potato, about 8 ounces, roughly chopped

2 zucchini, chopped

2½ cups water

4 ounces sorrel, torn

large handful of fresh chervil

large handful of fresh flat-leaf parsley

large handful of fresh mint

1 round or butterhead lettuce, separated into leaves

2½ cups vegetable stock

1 small head of radicchio

1 teaspoon peanut oil

salt and ground black pepper

Serves 4–6

4 Cook the radicchio wedges for 1 minute on each side until slightly charred. Reheat the soup over low heat, then ladle it into warmed shallow bowls. Serve a wedge of charred radicchio on top of each.

cock-a-leekie
with puy lentils and thyme

An ancient Scottish soup, originally made with veal to flavor the broth, this version is given more earthiness by Puy lentils.

1 Bring a small saucepan of salted water to a boil and cook the julienne of leeks for 1–2 minutes. Drain and refresh under cold running water. Drain again and set aside.

2 Pick over the lentils to check for any small stones or grit. Put into a saucepan with the bay leaf and thyme and cover with cold water. Bring to a boil and cook for 25–30 minutes, until tender. Drain and refresh under cold water.

3 Put the chicken breasts in a saucepan and pour over enough stock to cover them. Bring to a boil and poach gently for 15–20 minutes, until tender. Using a draining spoon, remove the chicken from the stock and let cool.

4 When the chicken is cool enough to handle, cut it into strips. Return it to the stock in the pan and add the lentils and the remaining stock. Bring just to a boil and add seasoning to taste.

5 Divide the leeks and prunes among four warmed bowls. Ladle over the hot chicken and lentil broth. Garnish each portion with a few fresh thyme sprigs and serve immediately.

cook's tip
To cut fine and even julienne strips, cut the leek into 2-inch lengths. Cut each piece in half lengthwise, then with the cut-side down, cut the leeks into thin strips.

you will need

2 leeks, cut into 2-inch fine julienne

½ cup Puy lentils

1 bay leaf

few sprigs of fresh thyme

2 skinless, boneless chicken breasts

3¾ cups good chicken stock

8 prunes, cut into strips

salt and ground black pepper

fresh thyme sprigs, to garnish

Serves 4

chicken and crab noodle soup
with cilantro omelet

The chicken makes a delicious stock for this light noodle soup with its illusive hint of enticing aromatic Chinese flavors.

1 Put the chicken and water in a pan. Bring to a boil, reduce the heat and cook gently for 20 minutes; skim the surface occasionally.

2 Slice half the scallions and add to the pan with the ginger, peppercorns, garlic and salt to taste. Cover and simmer for 1½ hours.

3 Meanwhile, soak the noodles in boiling water for 4 minutes or according to the package instructions. Drain and refresh under cold water. Shred the remaining scallions and set aside.

4 To make the omelets, beat the eggs with the cilantro and seasoning. Heat a little of the olive oil in a small frying pan.

5 Add a third of the egg and swirl the pan to coat the bottom evenly. Cook for 1 minute. Flip over and cook for 30 seconds. Turn the omelet out onto a plate and let cool. Repeat twice more to make three omelets. Roll up the omelets tightly one at a time and slice thinly.

6 Remove the chicken from the stock and let cool. Strain the stock through a muslin-lined sieve into a clean pan. When the chicken is cool enough to handle, remove and finely shred the meat, discarding the bones.

7 Bring the stock to a boil. Add the noodles, chicken, scallions and crabmeat, then simmer for 1–2 minutes. Stir in the soy sauce and season. Ladle the soup into bowls and top each with sliced omelet and cilantro leaves.

you will need

2 chicken legs, skinned
7½ cups cold water
large bunch of scallions
1-inch piece fresh ginger root, sliced
1 teaspoon black peppercorns
2 garlic cloves, halved
3 ounces rice noodles
4 ounces fresh white crabmeat
2 tablespoons light soy sauce
salt and ground black pepper
cilantro leaves, to garnish

FOR THE CILANTRO OMELETS
4 eggs
2 tablespoons chopped cilantro leaves
1 tablespoon extra virgin olive oil

Serves 6

fava bean, snow pea and spinach minestrone

you will need

2 tablespoons olive oil

2 onions, finely chopped

2 garlic cloves, finely chopped

2 carrots, very finely chopped

1 celery stalk, very finely chopped

5⅔ cups boiling water

1 pound shelled fresh fava beans

8 ounces snow peas, cut into fine strips

3 tomatoes, peeled and chopped

1 teaspoon tomato paste

2 ounces spaghettini, broken into
1½-inch lengths

8 ounces baby spinach

2 tablespoons chopped fresh parsley

handful of fresh basil leaves

salt and ground black pepper

basil sprigs, to garnish

freshly grated Parmesan cheese, to serve

Serves 6

The classic, wintry Italian minestrone soup takes on a summer-fresh image in this light recipe. Any small pasta shapes can be used instead of the spaghettini, if you prefer.

1 Heat the oil in a saucepan and add the onions and garlic. Cook for 4–5 minutes, until softened. Add the carrots and celery, and cook for 2–3 minutes. Add a boiling water and simmer for 15 minutes, until the vegetables are tender.

2 Cook the fava beans in boiling salted water for 4–5 minutes. Remove with a slotted spoon, refresh under cold water and set aside.

3 Bring the pan of water back to a boil, add the snow peas and cook for 1 minute, until just tender. Drain, then refresh under cold water and set aside.

4 Add the tomatoes and the tomato paste to the soup. Cook for 1 minute. Purée two or three large ladlefuls of the soup and a quarter of the fava beans in a food processor or blender until smooth. Set aside.

5 Add the spaghettini to the remaining soup and cook for 6–8 minutes, until tender. Stir in the purée and spinach and cook for 2–3 minutes. Add the rest of the fava beans, the snow peas and parsley, and season well.

6 When you are ready to serve the soup, stir in the basil leaves and ladle the soup into deep cups or bowls and garnish with sprigs of basil. Serve a little grated Parmesan with the soup.

avgolemono

This light and refreshing soup from Greece is very quick and simple to make. For the very best flavor use a well-flavored homemade chicken stock.

you will need

5 cups chicken stock

4 large eggs

juice of 2 large lemons

salt and ground black pepper

fresh chives, to garnish

Serves 4

1 Pour the chicken stock into a large saucepan and bring it slowly to a boil. Meanwhile, break the eggs into a large bowl and thoroughly whisk in the lemon juice.

2 Cool the stock very slightly, then thoroughly whisk a little into the egg and lemon mixture. Pour the lemon and egg mixture back into the main batch of stock and cook over very low heat, stirring continuously, until the soup is slightly thickened. Do not let the mixture boil.

3 Taste the soup and season lightly if required, then ladle into warmed bowls. Cut the chives into short lengths and sprinkle a few pieces on top of each portion. Serve immediately.

cook's tip

It is important to cook this delicate soup very gently over low heat, stirring constantly with a wooden spoon. Don't let it boil, or it will curdle. The soup is best eaten as soon as it is made.

roasted garlic soup with poached egg and croutons

you will need

1 tablespoon olive oil

1 bulb garlic, unpeeled and broken into cloves

4 slices day-old ciabatta bread, broken into pieces

5 cups chicken stock

pinch of saffron threads

1 tablespoon white wine vinegar

4 eggs

salt and ground black pepper

chopped fresh parsley, to garnish

FOR THE POLENTA

3 cups milk

1 cup quick-cook polenta

¼ cup butter

Serves 4

Spanish soup and Italian polenta marry wonderfully well in this recipe. The delicious garlic soup originates from Andalucia in Spain.

1 Preheat the oven to 400°F. Brush the olive oil on the inside of a roasting pan, then add the garlic and bread, and roast for about 20 minutes. Let sit until cool enough to handle.

2 Meanwhile, make the polenta. Bring the milk to a boil in a large, heavy pan and gradually pour in the polenta, stirring constantly. Cook for 5 minutes or according to the package instructions, stirring frequently, until the polenta begins to come away from the side of the pan.

3 Spoon onto a cutting board and spread out to about ½ inch thick. Let cool and set.

4 Squeeze the softened garlic cloves from their skins into a food processor or blender. Add the dried bread and 1¼ cups of the stock, then process until smooth. Pour into a saucepan. Pound the saffron to a powder in a mortar and stir in a little of the remaining stock, then add to the soup with enough of the remaining stock to thin the soup to the consistency you desire.

5 Cut the polenta into ½-inch dice. Melt the butter in a frying pan and cook the polenta over high heat for 1–2 minutes, tossing until beginning to brown. Drain on paper towels.

6 Season the soup and reheat gently. Bring a large frying pan of water to a boil. Add the vinegar and reduce the heat to a simmer. Crack an egg onto a saucer. Swirl the water with a knife and drop the egg into the middle of the swirl. Repeat with the remaining eggs and poach them for 2–3 minutes, until just set. Lift out the eggs using a draining spoon, then place one in each of four bowls. Ladle the soup over them, sprinkle polenta croutons and parsley on top and serve.

mediterranean seafood soup with saffron rouille

Vary the fish content of this soup according to the freshest available, but choose firm varieties that will not flake and fall apart easily during cooking.

1 Discard any open clams that do not shut when tapped sharply. Place the rest in a large saucepan with the wine. Cover and cook over high heat for 4 minutes, until the shells have opened.

2 Drain the clams, strain their cooking liquid and set it aside. Discard any unopened shells and reserve 8 clams in their shells. Remove the remaining clams from their shells and set aside.

3 Heat the oil in a pan. Add the garlic, fennel seeds and chile flakes and cook for about 2 minutes, until softened. Add the fennel, pepper, tomatoes, onion and cooking liquid. Cover and cook gently for 10 minutes, stirring occasionally.

4 Stir in the potatoes, bay leaf and thyme, then pour in the fish stock. Cover and cook for 15–20 minutes, until the vegetables are tender.

5 Meanwhile, make the saffron rouille. Pound the saffron threads to a powder in a mortar, then beat into the mayonnaise with the Tabasco. Cut the French bread into eight thin slices and toast them on both sides. Set aside.

6 Add the monkfish, red snapper and Pernod to the soup and cook for 3–4 minutes, until tender. Add the all the clams (with and without shells) and heat through for 30 seconds. Remove the bay leaf and thyme sprigs, and season the soup well. Spoon the rouille onto the toasts. Ladle the soup into bowls, garnish each bowl with a frond of fennel and serve with the toasts.

you will need

1 pound fresh clams, scrubbed

½ cup white wine

1 tablespoon olive oil

4 garlic cloves, crushed

1 teaspoon fennel seeds

pinch of dried chile flakes

1 fennel bulb, halved, cored and sliced

1 red bell pepper, seeded and sliced

8 plum tomatoes, halved

1 onion, cut into thin wedges

8 ounces small waxy potatoes, sliced

1 bay leaf

1 sprig fresh thyme

2½ cups fish stock

1 mini French bread

8 ounces monkfish fillet, sliced

12 ounces red snapper, scaled, filleted and cut into wide strips

3 tablespoons Pernod

1 small loaf French bread

salt and ground black pepper

fennel fronds, to garnish

FOR THE ROUILLE

a few saffron threads

⅔ cup mayonnaise

dash of Tabasco

Serves 4

the basics

Anyone can make soup. Kitchen novices and experienced cooks alike can be sure of success. While there are no hidden secrets or magic tricks, remembering a few simple techniques will make every soup assignment run just a little bit smoother.

making stocks

You can make great soups without fresh stocks, but stock-making is simple, quick and cheap. Stock will bubble unattended, leaving you free to get on with other things, then, when strained, skimmed and cooled, it freezes well. A good way to freeze stock is in 2½-cup batches. Line a deep plastic container with a freezer bag, leaving plenty of bag overhanging the side. Pour in the stock and cover the container. Freeze until solid, then remove the bag of frozen stock from the container, and seal and label the bag. Blocks of frozen stock can be stacked neatly in the freezer, and the containers can be used for other purposes.

The following are basic recipes, but you can add more or less what you like to stock. Clean vegetable peelings and stalks from fresh herbs will all add flavor to stocks, and this is also a good way of using up every part of the vegetable.

chicken stock

Use cold water to start the stock and heat it gently. Remember to skim off the scum, which would otherwise taint and cloud the stock.

you will need

2 pounds chicken bones and/or chicken wings

2 leeks, roughly chopped

1 large carrot, roughly chopped

1 celery stalk, roughly chopped

1 bay leaf

6 black peppercorns

2 sprigs fresh thyme

7½ cups cold water

Makes about 6¼ cups

1 Put all the ingredients into a large saucepan. Bring slowly to a boil, then use a spoon to skim off the scum.

2 Reduce the heat and simmer the stock very gently for 2–3 hours, skimming the surface occasionally to remove any scum. It is important to simmer the stock gently, as rapid boiling will make the stock cloudy.

3 Let cool slightly, then strain through a fine sieve (line with muslin if the sieve is not fine). Cool the stock, then chill it for up to 3 days or freeze.

fish stock

Preparing fish stock is the exception to the usual long-cooking rule, as it should simmer for just 20 minutes. Longer simmering will give a bitter flavor, but the strained stock can be cooked again, if you wish, to reduce its volume and concentrate the flavor. Use only the bones of white fish, such as sole, flounder or haddock. You can include heads, but remove the eyes and gills which will spoil the flavor of the stock.

you will need

3–3½ pounds fish bones, washed

2 large onions, roughly chopped

1 large leek, roughly chopped

1 celery stalk, roughly chopped

6 button mushrooms, sliced

6 black peppercorns

a few fresh parsley stalks

5 cups cold water

Makes about 5 cups

1 Cut large bones into two or three pieces and place in a large pan. Add the vegetables, peppercorns and parsley stalks. Pour in the water, bring to a boil, then skim. Reduce the heat and simmer for 20 minutes.

2 Strain the stock through a muslin-lined sieve and let sit until just cool. Chill for up to 3 days or freeze.

vegetable stock

Treat this recipe as a rough guide to making vegetable stock; you can also add any trimmings or peelings to contribute flavor. Just make sure everything is washed. Strongly flavored vegetables, such as rutabaga, cabbage and parsnips, that may dominate the flavor of the stock and are usually avoided. They can be added if you want a particularly full-flavored result, but remember to make a note of this on the label when freezing the stock, so that you know which dishes to use it in later. Root vegetables such as potatoes tend to make the stock cloudy.

you will need

1 large onion, roughly chopped

1 large leek, roughly chopped

2 carrots, sliced

1 celery stalk, roughly chopped

2 garlic cloves

8 white peppercorns

a few fresh parsley stalks

1 bay leaf

2 sprigs fresh thyme

5 cups cold water

Makes about 5 cups

1 Put all the ingredients in a large saucepan. Bring to a boil and skim off the scum that rises to the surface, then reduce the heat and simmer for 1 hour, skimming occasionally.

2 Strain the stock through a fine strainer (line the strainer with muslin if it is not very fine) and let sit until just cool. Chill for up to 3 days or freeze.

meat stock

This stock can be made using beef, veal or lamb bones. It gains a good strong flavor and color from roasting the bones. If you want to make ham stock follow this recipe, but do not roast the bones and omit the tomato paste.

you will need

3–3½ pounds beef, veal or lamb bones

1 large onion, unpeeled and quartered

1 large leek, roughly chopped

2 carrots, sliced

1 celery stalk, roughly chopped

2 tablespoons tomato paste

1 fresh bouquet garni

6 black peppercorns

13 cups cold water

Makes about 11 cups

1 Preheat the oven to 450°F. Put the bones in a roasting pan and roast them for 20 minutes. Add the vegetables, stir well and roast for another 20 minutes. Transfer the bones and vegetables to a large saucepan, then pour a little hot water into the roasting pan and stir well.

2 Place the roasting pan on the stove and heat, stirring continuously, until boiling. Scrape the sticky residue off the roasting pan and boil for 2–3 minutes, until all the residue is dissolved in the water. Add this to the saucepan.

3 Add the remaining ingredients. Bring to a boil and skim off the scum. Reduce the heat and simmer for 3 hours, skimming occasionally.

4 Strain the stock through a fine strainer and let sit until just cool. Chill for up to 3 days or freeze.

techniques and equipment

chopping an onion

Use a small knife to trim the root end of the onion and remove the skin with the tough layer underneath. Cut the onion in half. Place the cut-side down on a cutting board and use a large knife to slice down through the onion without cutting through the root. Slice horizontally through the onion. Finally, cut down across the original cuts and the onion will fall apart into fine dice.

peeling vegetables

The quickest way to peel vegetables is to use a swivel peeler. For example, trim off the top and end of a carrot, then hold the carrot in one hand and run the peeler away from you down its length, turning the carrot as you work.

cooking vegetables

Use a heavy saucepan to cook or sweat chopped vegetables. A good pan that conducts and holds heat well lets the vegetables cook for longer before browning, so that they can be softened without changing color.

cooking soups

Use a wooden spoon to stir soups at all stages of cooking. This will not damage the bottom of the saucepan (important if the pan is nonstick). However, wood absorbs flavors, so wash and dry the spoon well after use. And don't leave the spoon in the soup while it is cooking.

whisking

A balloon whisk is essential for quickly incorporating ingredients such as eggs and cream, which could curdle, or flour mixtures that can form lumps.

sieving soups

A wooden mushroom (or champignon), which looks like a large, flat toadstool) is useful for pressing ingredients efficiently through a fine sieve to give a smooth purée. The back of a large spoon or ladle also works, but it is a little slower.

puréeing soups

A hand-held blender is helpful, as it lets you blend the soup directly in the saucepan. Controlling the speed is easy to give the desired consistency.

A more traditional method is to use a Mouli-legume, a type of mechanical sieve. This sits over a bowl and has a blade to press the food through two fine sieves. The blade is turned by hand to push the soup through the sieves, leaving all the fibers and solids behind.

The most common items of equipment for puréeing soups are food processors and free-standing blenders. Both types of machine are quick and efficient, but the food processor does not produce as smooth a result as a conventional blender, and for some recipes the soup will need to be sieved afterwards.

Food processors can also be used for finely chopping and slicing vegetables for salsas and garnishes as well as for the soup itself.

cook's tip
Remember to avoid overfilling a food processor or blender, as liquid can seep out from around the blade or through the lid. Most soups will need to be processed in two or three batches.

thickening soups

beurre manié

This smooth flour and butter paste is used to thicken soups at the end of the cooking time. Equal amounts of flour and butter are kneaded together, then a small pat of the paste is added to the soup and whisked until it is fully incorporated before the next is added. The soup is brought to a boil and simmered for about 1 minute, until thickened and to avoid a raw flour flavor. A similarly useful paste can be made using flour and cream.

cream

Heavy cream can be used to thicken a fine soup. It is added toward the end of cooking, then the soup is brought to a boil and simmered gently for a few minutes until the soup is slightly reduced and thickened.

cornstarch or arrowroot

These fine flours are mixed with a little cold water (about double the volume of the dry ingredient) to make a smooth, thick, but runny, paste. (This is known as

slaking.) The paste is stirred into the hot soup and simmered, stirring, until thickened. Cornstarch takes about 3 minutes to thicken completely and lose its raw flavor. Arrowroot achieves maximum thickness upon boiling and tends to become slightly thinner if it is allowed to simmer for any length of time, so this is usually avoided. Cornstarch gives an opaque result, but arrowroot becomes clear when it boils, so it is useful for thickening clear liquids.

bread crumbs

The more rustic approach is to use fresh white bread crumbs to thicken soup. Simply stir the bread crumbs into the finished soup and simmer briefly.

eggs

Beaten eggs, egg yolks, or a mixture of eggs and a little cream can be used to enrich and slightly thicken a smooth soup. Whisk the eggs or egg and cream into the hot soup, but do not let it boil once added or they will curdle.

flavoring soups

herbs

Stirring chopped fresh herbs into a finished soup can add a wealth of flavor as well as color. Add them just before serving, as they lose their potency when cooked. Opt for soft-leafed herbs, such as basil, flat-leaf parsley, chervil, dill, mint and chives. Woody herbs, such as rosemary and thyme, are best cooked in a soup in the early stages.

oils and vinegars

Flavored oils and vinegars are useful for splashing into finished soups to pack an extra punch. Consider chili oil for a super-fiery flavor in a spicy soup, or basil or arugula oil to enliven a fish or Mediterranean-style soup. Infuse virgin olive oil with chiles, roasted whole garlic cloves, whole spices, woody herbs or citrus peel instead of buying aromatic flavored oil. Flavor and color oil with soft herbs, such as basil, following the method for Tomato, Ciabatta and Basil Oil Soup.

Vinegar adds bite to some soups, so look for the many types available, including wine vinegars, balsamic vinegar, sherry vinegar and fruit-flavored vinegars, such as raspberry.

alcohol

Add to soups in moderation. The golden rule is to simmer the soup for a few minutes to cook off the strong alcohol, leaving the flavor. White wine, Pernod and vermouth work very well with creamy fish soups. Some spirits, such as vodka, can be used in chilled soups.

flavored creams

These provide a wonderful way of introducing contrasting flavor to a finished soup. Crème fraîche or whipped heavy cream can be transformed by adding a homemade purée of fresh herbs, roasted peppers or sun-dried tomatoes. Infused saffron and homemade pesto are also delicious additions.

sauces

For those who like very hot food, chili sauce can be offered at the table. Thai fish sauce (*nam pla*) is a seasoning and condiment, which is used in much the same way as soy sauce in Chinese cooking; it can be added to soup just before eating to add a punchy flavor.

Pesto and pistou are closely related, the latter hailing from southern France, where it is stirred into a rich vegetable soup. Both are made by mixing crushed garlic, basil and olive oil, and pesto has pine nuts and Parmesan cheese added. Stir into soup or spread on toasted bread and float on top of the soup.

Mayonnaise is a good medium for introducing other flavors, such as garlic, chili, saffron, purées of leafy herbs, spinach, arugula, fennel or Pernod.

Flavored butters can be spread on warm bread or hot toast to accompany a soup or simply added to each bowl of soup just before serving. Flavorings range from herbs and spices to shellfish.

garnishes

herbs

Adding a handful of chopped fresh herbs to a bowl of soup just before serving it can make a good soup look great. Use herb flowers in the summer months—for example, try rosemary, marjoram or thyme.

Fried herbs make an unusual garnish and they add a crisp texture to soup. Deep-fry herb leaves in hot oil for a few seconds, then drain on paper towels. Parsley, basil and sage all work well.

A bundle of chives makes a dainty garnish. Cut 5–6 chives to about 2¹/₂ inches long and tie them in a bundle using another length of chive.

fried croutons and bread crumbs

These classic garnishes add texture as well as flavor. To make croutons, cut bread into small cubes and fry the cubes in a little oil. Toss the bread continuously so that the cubes are golden all over,

then drain on paper towels. The same method is used for fresh bread crumbs, but the cooking time is shorter. You can use any bread, from whole-grain to ciabatta, or walnut to sun-dried tomato, and it is a good way of using up a slightly stale loaf. Flavor croutons or bread crumbs with chopped fresh herbs or spices, or by stirring in a tablespoon of sesame seeds, sliced almonds or poppy seeds just before they finish cooking.

broiled croûtes

Topped with cheese, croûtes not only look good, but taste great in all kinds of soups. To make them, toast small slices of baguette on both sides. If desired, you can rub the toast with a cut clove of garlic, then top with grated Cheddar or Parmesan, a crumbled blue cheese, such as Stilton, or a slice of goat cheese. Then broil briefly until the cheese is just beginning to melt. Float one or two croûtes on the bowls of soup.

chips

Use these to add a crisp dimension to smooth and rustic soups. Try shop-bought thick-cut chips or tortilla chips; alternatively, make your own vegetable chips. Wafer-thin slices of fresh raw beets, pumpkin or parsnips can all be deep-fried in hot oil for a few moments to produce delicious chips.

salsas

Raw salsa mixtures also add vivid colors and flavors to soups. Try different combinations of finely diced vegetables, such as tomatoes, onions (red or white), cucumbers and avocados, and combine with chopped or sliced chiles, corn kernels and chopped fresh herbs.

vegetable julienne

An effective way of preparing ingredients for adding a splash of color to soup is to cut them into julienne strips. Shreds of scallions or red and green chiles make great garnishes. Alternatively, finely dice peeled and seeded tomatoes.

crisp-fried shallots

Finely sliced shallots or small red onions make a quick and flavorful garnish for smooth lentil and vegetable soups. Cut them crosswise into rings, then shallow-fry in hot oil or a mixture of butter and oil until crisp and golden. Scallions can also be used, simply cut lengthwise into fine shreds before frying.

cream and yogurt

A swirl of cream is the simplest soup garnish and is good for smooth soups. If the soup is very thin, then whip the cream lightly so that it floats. Alternatively whip the cream until it holds soft peaks and drop a dollop into the center of the soup. Spoonfuls of crème fraîche and plain yogurt can also be used for a garnish.

index